# WE ARE BRAVER THAN WE KNOW

*Poems and writings penned during the covid pandemic, lockdowns and beyond...*

MIRA MIDHA

INDIA • SINGAPORE • MALAYSIA

ISBN

Hardcase 979-8-89363-963-6
Paperback 979-8-89363-408-2

Dedicated to my grandson, my 'Champ'……
"Dearest Aditya, this one is for you."

# Index

The scenes and people I have written about are so 'there' yet not there. It is convenient to overlook their presence so they fade into obscurity.

I try not to write mere words but capture the ethos of images in every line of my poetry. Tired souls silent but speaking. Each poem is a reality, every poetry a photograph, carving an enduring memory in the mind of the reader.

# Preface....

One may move or be still
But you will go forward....
Because time travels ahead
And it takes you along....
This life is a journey....
We are all in it together....
Yet....
Each one's journey is their own....

During the covid pandemic, the world became silent. It was a silence that had a sound. The earth went through a change.
We lost....lived....fell....we rose....
We waited at the door and then started again....
Took a deep breath and then let go....

The lockdowns became a time of contemplation for me. Many of my poems, in this book, reflect my thoughts and verses resonate with emotions of many an ordeal and misfortunes as well as the process of slow healing. This time of isolation made me deliberate on life and its meaning. It made me prioritize and realize there was so much I could do without and still be happy. There was also a quietness within and this subtle realization was almost meditative.

At the same time, we had all become so vulnerable and the lack of protection from what was happening around us, was just not in our control. There were hard moments. Nothing was going as intended. Amid all this, life was still progressing in a staggered way. Yet, my eyes and feelings hurt every time I looked out and felt a sadness, a helplessness. Everything was empty. People had disappeared. The message was one of apprehension about this abnormal, unreal situation. The only way out was to go through it. Layers and layers. A work in progress. Come along on this journey with me.........

# *A Quietness of Self.....*

Shy are the unsaid words,
Voices without sound,
Without breath....
Intense and deep,
A stillness, a peace...
I rejoice in my solitude,
My calm...
Only the brave
Dare to tread where
The hush is so profound....
Voices without sound....
Without breath.....

I can see your thoughts....
In a distant there,
Your looking towards nowhere,
And echoes of words in a silence
That speaks....
Eventually, all feelings pass,
Even though there may be darkness,
Somehow life goes on....
Because there is light somewhere else....

*****

# *Introduction....*

***'Lockdown'.... notes to myself....***
***The beginning....***

We opened our eyes to a bleak silence. Empty streets, closed offices, shops, and schools. The entire nation had come to a standstill as a result of this covid spiral.

Many of those who fell into this humanitarian crisis still remain jobless and food insecure. The climb upward has been difficult. Everyone was gripped by an alien nervousness. This pandemic resulted in terrible fear. A lot of households were economically crippled as a consequence of this. So many people were grieving the loss of loved ones. It seemed, at times, like a nightmare from a science fiction movie. The only difference was that this was not a movie; this was the real thing!

**29th March 2020**

It seems like 'glitter rain', with the sun playing peek-a-boo. I don't remember it raining so much in March....third evening of thunder, rain and yesterday, hailstones....a natural cleansing of the air I hope....

**30th March 2020**
My kitchen window....
It's a busy area, my kitchen, yet this little sunbird is building a nest on the stems of the climbing ivy that is entwining in and out of the wrought iron grill. Intriguing weaver, this tiny, frantic, fluttering bird. Nature seems to have found confidence in this space, sans human interventions. Maybe the silence in the atmosphere has given it a newfound freedom.

Today was day one of nest-building.

**31st March 2020**
Further to my yesterday's post....

This little sunbird is one helluva quick builder. What a comfortable and cozy nest. I love the shape and the aesthetics that have gone into it and am extremely careful while clicking. I don't want to disturb it.

**8th April 2020**
Sitting on my sofa, a little tired after the day's housework and cooking, my mind is reflecting on the very sad and alarming situation everywhere. I could only say a prayer. Then I saw a small beam of light through drawn curtains shine on a painting of Lord Buddha facing me "A light of hope."
"Maybe," I thought to myself.

**9th April 2020**
I'm waiting, looking up and out. The sky is a clear blue, and everything is so serene.

We are entering another lockdown as this shutdown draws to an end. I am okay.

I remember feeling uneasy about the prospect of being confined with all the work, but I have adjusted and come to terms with it.

These days, my world is my home. The day starts and ends here. For the time being, there is no beyond. Just what is required and nothing more is our primary focus, and I know this is adequate. A silent togetherness has brought about a compatible comfort. My husband and I work in rhythmic harmony.

I've become aware of the minor details that I earlier took for granted and understand their significance. I now tackle all tasks with affection and attention to detail. I have the patience and the time. Being calm is so soothing. As I gradually accept, adjust, and change, mundane tasks are now therapeutic as opposed to tedious or tiresome.

If you are unable to alter it, accept it.

Make the necessary adjustments so that it fits into your life and way of thinking.

As much as you can, evolve with the situation so that you can move on.

This has turned into my catchphrase.

What really matters is my family, my home, our health, and our peace of mind. If used effectively, the rest is a nice extra. I am content, and we are content. For now, that is enough to see us through.

**16th April 2020**

Dearest Aditya, HAPPY BIRTHDAY, my jaan. Thirteen years....you are officially a teenager. NOW THE FUN BEGINS....

We are feeling so bad that we can't cut a cake with you because of this lockdown, but once it's lifted, we shall CELEBRATE. Love you lots....Nani, Nana.

**23rd April 2020**

At the moment, the alternatives are very few. Behind closed doors....clean, cook, read, listen to music, watch television, use social media and occasionally look out. Pune has gone silent. A little update on the sunbirds.....I thought they too had gone into lockdown. I hadn't seen the pair for a while but realized, mum was incubating and dad was keeping a hidden vigil.

I think the chicks have arrived. There is a sudden 'bobbing' activity at the opening of the nest by mother, feeding, while dad issues noisy warnings, hopping from branch to branch at the sight of any disturbance.

**2nd May 2020**

Heavy rain and strong gusty winds. I saw the tiny nest swinging like a pendulum. I had to give it some support, so used the palm of my hand as a shield. Hope the little ones are safe. Will know when mum comes to feed in the morning.

**3rd May 2020**

Babes are okay. I can hear their chirps and mama bird is doing what she usually does, flying....fetching....feeding. Dad is being as cautious as ever. He has a loud voice for such a tiny bird and keeps us away from the window.

**4th May 2020**

I spent the majority of this afternoon removing leaves from a small flower bed. Such a mass had accumulated. The Jack fruit tree is shedding so many leaves, and so quickly!

Even though it was hot and humid and I had a headache, I was unwilling to sit down and watch the news, another movie, or anything else on television.

I was also done with the house cleaning. My initial enthusiasm for squeezing into nooks and crannies had vanished. Yes, the zeal and vigour with which I had attacked the housework had faded and I had once again overdone the leaf raking. A mild painkiller helped and....what now? There is so much time on hand and nowhere to go!

Somebody said to try a few new dishes. Cooking!! I have never cooked so much, ever. Not only that, I have just got overfull from smelling all the meals I have stirred that my hunger has vanished.

Tried to keep the flag of cheer and optimism flying high during the initial lockdown and maybe halfway through the second one but the 'yeah' feeling is kind of wearing out. I just need to have faith that everything will work out sooner rather than later. I suppose everyone is experiencing the same anxiety. I have not stepped out of my house in so many days! To say that I am feeling very caged in is bit of an exaggeration but I am starting to feel claustrophobic. I am sure 'this too shall pass'....until then....

I'm making an effort to add some humour to my notes in order to make myself feel a little lighter. But the reality is that we are all feeling the impact of this isolation. Daily life is characterized by a mad rush to stock up and food hoarding, whenever stores are open. This is far from reality, and an annoying depression is taking hold. In the voices of those I speak with, I observe a sigh of 'giving up'. The narrative is, "We can't do this anymore."

The only source of entertainment, or perhaps I should say distraction, is the television. I struggle not to tap the news channel button, yet I do, in the hope of finding a positive update. But the images one sees are too upsetting and depressing.

**5th May 2020**

The lockdown was eased up enough for liquor retailers to open today. The disorder then got started in the midst of the morning. It was audible to me, because close to where I stay, there is a store. Police sirens were accompanied by an upsurge in the shouting. Now there is absolute silence.

The liquor stores are no longer open. Did the authorities concerned not think this activity would require discipline? Come on, perhaps it would have been wise to execute a little planning? I guess we're back to where we started once again.

**6th May 2020**

Sunbird update....

I was a bit worried after the storm....

But today two beaks were popping out....they are okay.

So, as the days passed, I stopped writing updates.

One morning, I looked down from my balcony. The silent road rose up to meet me and then I looked up at the sky, the sun shone to warm my face. The quietness was holistic and nature was having a lot of uninterrupted happy moments. A sigh left me. Beauty comes in very different ways. I was a bit tired, but not exhausted. I was apprehensive, but not too fearful. It had been a time of big changes and sometimes I wondered what it was going to mean for me and my family.

I had no answers. Whenever my husband coughed or sneezed, I would look at him in alarm. It passed....my fears were unreasonable, but times were unfamiliar.

I waited for the lockdown to end and it did.

We all emerged with a strong feeling of togetherness, learning from a situation out of our hands. A lot of severe lockdown measures had been introduced, such as school closure, social distancing, interruption of sports activities, and quarantine/isolation. These restrictive measures may have had serious psychological consequences for young and senior individuals, especially among the more vulnerable. It left most of us feeling overwhelmed and anxious. We had to remind ourselves over and over again that we were all adjusting to a new normal.

I came to understand that nothing is permanent. Anything can happen at any time. We frequently take for granted the people we love, our privileges, and our physical well-being. In my opinion, the lockdowns made us appreciate life and those around us, whether they be loved ones or unknown individuals. We all pursue work, money, fame, and occasionally overlook that we have family and friends who need our time too. We neglect the fact that we all have to give ourselves a break and slow down. Furthermore, many of us also found a strength or a side to ourselves that emerged in times of hardship, enabling us to fully demonstrate who we are.

As you read on, you will feel that many of my poems have a similar touch.... a continuation of thought, be it nature, personal, or poignant surroundings of everyday life. These are stirring sentiments and impressions and it makes me aware of the deep, meaningful ambience we live in. So I keep picking up threads of emotions, interwoven in the landscape around me and writing them down. Just as seasons change and spring births anew, so shall the stark, dreary winter end and a new day will dawn....

A carpet of dried leaves,
Fallen,

Covering a street
That speaks in silence
Of a change in season,
Nothing new....
Just a sense of life evolving....

Time passes into shadows
To become a past....
And a past gradually disappear
Into the earth,
Not a wrinkle on the ground....

*****

***Starlight did a fading...***
***The moon glow waved goodbye....***
***Dawn was now breaking,***
***Shadows dimmed in sighs....***
***Another night....another day,***
***I still chose to face the sun,***
***Rising coyly over yon horizon,***
***The dark had taken its run....***

*****

## *Kitchen Window Grill..... Peace Lilly....*

I stand gazing outside my kitchen window, admiring the Peace Lily plant swaying in the gentle breeze.

We all have our own small urban oasis where we relax and find our peace of mind. Ours is an old fashioned house with lots of heritage, old artefacts retaining their 'organic vintage' style and lots of new artefacts that look like 'old vintage'. Lots of plants. Lots and I mean lots of paintings (a bit of artistic clutter). An abundance of colour, sunlight, fresh air, bird songs, picturesque sunrises and sunsets. The small 'big' things we take for granted.

I love the inside and care a lot for the outside. I will fight, if I have to, for the cleanliness around me and save the amazing wealth in a variety of trees that surround us. Do we ever stop and notice? They house an entire eco-system within the leaves, bark and branches. I enjoy seeing the seamless flow of seasonal changes year after year, even when the rain throws things off. Yes, we live in a city with a lot of man-made problems and at times it makes no sense. There is a lot of chaos out there, but there is also a haven one can create where everything makes sense.

There is a space
Between the earth
And the sky
Where we unite....
There shall be light,
Passing to the other side of the walls,
As generations walk across....
Enveloping joys and pain,
Celebrating, reminiscing moments
Of laughter....old stories....
Moving on past the shadow
And sunlight,
Through doors, windows,
Along with emotions
And so much more in a roam,
Embracing the new
Then a comfortable old....
This place is called our home....
There is a space
Between the earth
And the sky
Where we unite....

* * * * *

# POETRY AND MORE....
# Ink on Paper,
# Retracing My Thoughts....

### *Gratitude....*

I thank you for that handshake,
I thank you for that smile,
I thank you for each day,
That makes it worth my while,
I need to count my blessings,
I need to value the good things,
I need to understand that luck is
A toss of coin,
When flipped, it takes wings....
Not to fly away but land on the floor,
I need to understand that there are just two sides,
And I could never ask for more....
'Cause one side is just the other,
Either which way you choose,
The mind has picked your inner wish,
You never win or lose....
So....
I thank you for that handshake,

I thank you for that smile,
I thank you for each day,
That makes it worth my while....

*****

## *Pray for Those Still Standing....*

My eyes are still aching from the scenes we all witnessed during the covid pandemic.... flaming pyres, dead floating in rivers and the wails and cries of people desperate to save their loved ones. So many died suddenly, leaving bereaved families. It was just too tragic. However, some people benefited from these monumental disasters. How did their conscience and morality transform them into such people? I am still wondering if humans have a dark, hidden side that we are not aware of.

Pray not for me
But for my unquiet soul....
Lost in the cries of mothers
And wails of a child....
Lost in the burning pyres wild
That consume the concrete below....
Melted in the pain and woe
Of mere mortals.

Pray not for me....
I am gone....
For I have found a peaceful place
Between sunset and dawn....
Pray for those who are still standing,
Their heart heavy with lust
For power....for their blindness....
They laugh with a grotesque
Evil sound and rub their palms,
Feasting like predators
On devastation and harm.

How did we come to this?
Where land was but a funeral ground,
And all around
Prostrated beings begging
For a gasp of air,
That was everywhere....
Once....our birth right....
Now suffocated by those who dole
A portion....
Smothered in the smog and smoke
Of flames that weep of lost hope....
She sits alone...eyes vacant,
Limbs too shattered to move....
For this was not his time....
Nor the way to go….
Gasping....choking slow....

Pray not for me....
For I am gone....
Pray for those still standing....

*****

## *Waiting for Better Days*

Here I stand looking into a vast,
The blue blemished by
Sprouts of grey clouds,
Slipping away, yet casting
An omen of a gathering storm,
And the world turns,
Putting on a show after show.

Fire wrapped, the setting sun,
The golden hour,
Navigating the trials of time....
Sends a slight shiver....
Is it a second sight,
A soothsaying of days to come?
'Nay....' I shake my head
And see it as a forecast,
Divinity casts a glow of magic.

Yet.......
A distant thunder...it's rumbling
In a portentous muffled loud,
As my eyes blankly stare,
Into where
I try and deceive my mind
Into a trance of 'all is well'....

My feet, grounded in this little open space,
Brows knitted, hands clasping a hot cuppa,
Clothes in a careless crease and....

My back slightly weary, with
An annoying tug that was never there.
It's quiet....

Few sounds of children next door,
An odd cawing of the crow,
And grateful to the koel
Who sings, perhaps, the sadness away,
To better days....
Broken by intermittent
Dull rumbling of wheels,
On a distant road.

Sluggish in her walk,
A lady surrendering to the
Grim narrative of today's story,
Face concealed behind
An ominous mask,
That all but tells
A dismal tiding of our days....
I wonder, when will it all align,
Maybe just a sign
And it will all heal,
Leaving just ashes of yesterday.

"Where have we reached?" I ask myself....
Did all the years of seeing good,
Toiling to make a world of ease
And well-being, come to naught?
"Where do we go from here?"
I suddenly feel there are no answers,

The next day is not known....
My hand clasps the cup tighter,
A warmth spreads through the palm,
Where they say the future is told,
I stare at the lines....
If only I knew....

* * * * *

## ***Healing.....***

When all around is a loud unease,
And the quiet harbours'
An inauspicious fear,
Alas....a laughing child
I seldom hear....
Far above a wandering moon,
I sleep the song
Of a restless tune,
With stars that speak
Through darkened night,
I wait....we wait
For a light....
It's there....oh it's there,
Among the work of wings,
This, the early dawn, when they find
A reason to sing,
Of good tidings….

The softened grass
I am told....
Capture fallen blossoms
In its fold....
To infuse the earth
With a fragrance of hope and cheer,
So I lie enveloped in this aroma
And hear,

A hosanna and I cry,
For all unfortunate lapsed by....
Yet,
Now joyous of days not too far,
Of a reflection in the stars....
Let this be a healing....

*****

## *The Lonely Sparrow.....*

The lonely tree stood stark and still,
A winter coat of snow and chill,
Branches brittle, stretched in sleep,
Roots hibernating deep.

Forlorn, a mournful sparrow sang,
Soft chirp, a feeble echo rang,
In a dispirited cry, being where,
Not a bud or bloom resided there.

In want of nest to warm a cold,
Chirping got louder, bold,
But alas, in a glacial silence, mum,
Not a whimper, not a hum.

Night and day, the bird did sing,
A serenade, it thought, would bring
Other souls on this bough to perch,
Woe....eyes forever searched.

Now the stalwart tree through many a day,
Saw seasons turn, all found their way,
It shook in the breeze, last leaves did fall,
Nestling the bird till spring did call.

Twitters filled the tree, the branches beamed,
As hues of vibrant colours greened,
"Little sparrow," rugged tree whispered one morn,
"Nothing is lost....nothing's gone,
Sing your heart out, all is fine,
You see....everything has its time."

*****

## ***Soul Fragrance....***

In the reality of beings and things,
Lies an adventure of time....
The life it has led....
The fascinating journey of
The whole....the broken....
Then put back together,
To become an epic story with a soul....
And the fragrance of that soul
Forever lives on....

* * * * *

## *We All Bleed the Same.....*

There is life and there is death....
The only two truths of existence....
All else is of our own making.....
Results and consequences we bear....
'Tis only us....
There are many narratives
And I take no sides,
For we all bleed the same....
Our thoughts, our convictions, our beliefs,
Power, humility, religion, science....
What is right?
What is wrong?
The line is very thin....
We need to recognize the difference,
And guidance is always needed....
Pray in quiet,
Pray within,
Pray in faith....
Pray with love and not in fear....
Fear is an instrument of the exploiter,
And faith....
The blessings of the benevolent.

*****

## ***Observations of a Wandering Mind....***

I) Walls along the boundary of another side,
Still life of faces on a poster,
Stained and smeared,
Pasted among graffiti and
The tattered remnants
Of bygone news of another world,
On plaster peeled, bruised bricks
Of a notice board for the walking,
Illuminated by an uneasy glare
Of summer light, old stickers
Yellowed, brittle and tearing....
A shout in silence....
Textures in a unique creation,
Strewn across sprawling compounds,
In conversations beyond a pristine vicinity,
It is always heard by reclining backs,
And curious eyes, peering, absorbing,
Messages overlapping....
Some call it 'street art'....

II) Everyone, yet nobody,
In this big place of loneliness....
A broken slipper by the wayside,
Sudden shelter from the rain at night,
Now abandoned....
Prayers of petals on a lonely grave,
Souvenirs of somebody's presence....
Lost time but silently speaking....
Those within....look out in curiosity

At an altering world,
Eves dropping on the heartbeat
Of a sleeping dog in the sweltering
Afternoon heat, dreaming of winter,
Under the canopy of gold,
As the summertime laburnum blossom....
Everyone, yet nobody,
In this big city of loneliness....

III) We walk as we talk....
Reaching home....
Looking out at a dusky sky,
Sunset colours draped across
Windows....
Thinking back with a smile....
We had walked in that summer heat
For maybe a mile....
I remind myself....
Remember this, it will not come again....
This period of time....an hour or so,
But looking back,
The width of span was many years ago....
It seems like it was just yesterday,
So near yet so far,
Yet I can still feel a warmth of closeness,
That's what good memories are....

IV) Moving toward evening,
I listen to sounds on the outside,
An orchestra of many instruments....
The worker sweeping leaves off a driveway,

Swishing her broom along a concrete path,
An auto rickshaw backfiring....shattering the wind
That is picking up speed,
Jarring of loading and unloading girders
And a grinding of the earth, courtesy
A perennial onslaught of killing
The few urban green zones left….
My windows knock,
Who's there? Black clouds....
Ah, just a thunderstorm on the horizon....
Children on the street, screaming in
Gay abandon....
A small audience pays momentary heed
To their raucous game of cricket.
The mosque, not too far away, comes alive....
Five o'clock prayers in the background....
The air is sultry and warm,
Limbs lethargic....
It's tea time, but too hot
For a cup of chai,
Yet a ritual, maybe a sip or two less
Than normal....
The wind picks up momentum,
Branches dance and my windows
Drum along rhythmically....
It's going to rain,
Then all shall be silent, except
An onslaught accompanied by a barrage
Of berserk water drops gone wild....
It did so yesterday,
Bringing down trees....

Summer moves towards the monsoons,
Once again....

V) Red wine and old rose,
Piano lilts 'Fur Elise'....
Wood fire and crackling embers,
And I remember....
Till an amber dust turns to
A golden dawn....
Black birds sing
A morning song....
The meadows frost thaws to dew....
There....grazing sheep,
But a few....
A ghost behind cotton clouds,
Faint, a voice hushed in loud,
It stirs a feel within me....
As I close my eyes, only I can see,
There, there....and there....
Past moments brought alive everywhere....
I'm old but I too need
A lap to lay down my head and cry,
Don't go....
I miss you so....
Red wine and old rose,
Piano lilts 'Fur Elise'....
Wood fire and crackling embers,
And I remember....

VI) The day went slow....
Peace was an invisible

Still-life of inertia,
As the sky lost its scorching glow,
And became this cool blue ocean....
Time, tinted with rippling shadows,
Dotted with falling leaves,
As it pulsed on a wall with a heart,
Striking a visual of symbolic loneliness....
Who shall write this story
Of shedding summer blooms?
As chapters bury memories
Along the wall of a past....
It hurts to see these flowers leaving,
There is no solace from a dead tree....
Who shall write their obituary?

*****

## Forgotten Souls.....

I'm aware that extremely moving poems have been written about the men, women, and children who have travelled our roads and highways, braving all the terrible challenges and longing to return home. It's heartbreaking. I had to write a few words for them....

The roads....the travelled path,
Railroad tracks, blood stained with an aftermath,
Of tragedies and broken bones,
We fight this fight of the living dead,
We fight so....oh so alone.

I do not have the luxury to cry,
I do not have the luxury to eat,
I do not have the luxury to sit or stand,
I do not have the luxury to sleep.

My child is craving with parched lips,
My old mother braves pain, yet bides her way,
My pregnant wife lays down, writhing....
In this dirt and sodden soil, my little girl is born today.

I do not curse the gods....
The miles ahead is our wretched destiny,
If those who were thought to be our own,
Turn blind to this inhuman pain and do not see....

Though we gave up our home in search of a better life,
That we too live and breathe the same air,

And as we did toil to put shoes on our feet,
Remember, for you all who take respite,
Once we were there....we were there.

Now are we no one....just a mere burden?
An eyesore? Do not seek me with pity,
I ask no alms....I ask no largesse,
Just get me back home with dignity.

*****

## *Vintage....*

Amid all the noise,
Street vendors and distractions,
The gentle beauty of peeling paint,
Vintage rustic doors....
The old artistry of weathered wood
Slips us by....
Muted hues, half painted walls
Seldom catches the ordinary eye....
Until we look for those glimpses
Of hidden remains from another time,
They were once the soul of this town....
That town,
Now standing shy,
With an aroma of inspiration....
Oh, these delightful homes of old....

*****

## ***The Living World of Animal and Man......***

The air is fresh....
Something tells me the coast is clear
And there is a soothing silence....
Free from fear,

Dare I step out?
'Tis not my domain,
Nor
My habitat anymore....
Yet, I see uninhabited streets
And locked doors.

But as I shyly venture out,
Through foliage green....
I am awestruck....
Not a human to be seen.

Can I dance and idly graze?
Where have they all gone?
Amidst all this beauty of spring,
Am I truly alone?

I have been hiding,
Hiding....hiding to feel safe,
Yet now....
Everything is so beautiful,
Every little thing in its place.

The air seems cleaner
Than it has ever been,
And the waters clearer,
Than ever seen....

So....I am moving out on tiptoes....
Maybe....just maybe, as I reach out
And clasp your hand....
We can amicably share
This hallowed land.

* * * * *

## A Ray of Light......

Let's walk these miles together....
We have a long way to go….
You have burdens on your shoulders,
And so have I....
The scars have begun to show....
The soles beneath our feet tire in heavy,
As do our weary treads,
Have stalled many a time....
Though....
A heart has battled with the head....
Losing hope is a misfortune,
Belief has to be there....
For we have all shared
A feeling of anguish and that of despair….

Yet, a spirit heralds an optimism,
And it says with conviction,
There shall be rest,
Through every trial of fire,
We all strove to do our best.
Now....
Through all the heartbreak and angst,
We will move with grace,
To wash away this taint of unease,
Find a moment in this space,
Where we arrived....and we shall....
My friend....we shall....
The burdens shall turn to slight,
Weakness to a might,

Positivity shall fight the fear,
And all that is dear,
Will resound in the hallelujah
That we hear....
Good times may have gone,
But....
Bad times also do not last,
As the saying goes....
"This too shall pass."

*****

## A Man With No Name....

What we have in life is a dream for many.

Let us call him Ahmed. He sits on the side of a traffic light junction. A crossing so busy and at times chaotic, is no place for someone to sit and that too inches away from the main road. Why does he do that? How else would his arms reach out to the cars, bikes and auto rickshaws next to him? He reaches out for alms, dragging himself back and forth. Ahmed has no legs. He sits at this junction from morning to night. It is a rare sight not to see him there. A jaunty cap on his head and a smile on his face, he profusely blesses everyone who puts an offering into his hands. His words are prayers of thanks and gratefulness. If he is dodged or ignored, the smile never vanishes. His expressions show no disappointment or indignation. It is amazing for a human being to display such a large hearted response for having so little. Don't we, who have so much to be thankful for, shrink to a mere 'small' next to him?

We drive past him nearly every day and when the traffic signal is green, it is not possible to stop by him. Yet his eyes meet everyone and his happy face seems to say, "It's okay.... next time."

Was he born like this, or did he meet with an accident? It is a thought that runs through my mind each time I see him. I am sure he has seen better days, yet his present infirmities have put him on a long, long road from where there is no return.

It doesn't take too much for us to be kind and compassionate, but it takes a lot for him, who has no choice, to be brave. Ahmed teaches all who pass him a lesson.

A message or a truth gets embedded unknowingly in our conscience and we all silently say a prayer of gratitude for all we have.

*****

## *The Sage....Wise Words....*

I came upon a sage one day,
His serene smile said all
He had to say,
Without words, he spoke to me,
You shall be,
If only you would let yourself see....

Be around that feeling of warmth,
Laugh with all you love,
Light up your life
With the aura about....
Take out that strength in hiding,
We are stronger than we know.

Forgive yourself, and
Others for mistakes,
It clears our mind....
Something has to leave
For another to fill it....
We need that constructive space,
Do you feel lost at times?
Go slowly....
Rediscovering takes time,
Move at your pace,
Reach out when you are ready,
Create your own beginnings,
And your own closure....

*****

## *City Lights and Streets of Dilemma....*

City lights and streets of dilemma....
A lonely man's table,
Surrounded by fallen leaves....
Winter bareness mourns
Moments of utmost sadness,
Eclipsed by a season of joy as
Spring births in celebration....

The brown dog,
Curled on his sidewalk patch,
Unconcerned by the overflowing
Garbage of wasted trash....
Rancid and reeking….
Humans disregard for space
Beyond his house walls.

A rag picker on his morning rounds,
Gathering empty bottles
And disfigured plastic glasses,
Thrown without a care after a roadside binge,
His scant days earnings go
Into a night of inebriation....

We watch
As guardians of law look
The other way,
Deliberate in their ignorance of drunks
Near a liquor shop,
Who usurp squares of dirt plots,

Hands dipped in unpalatable morsels,
Fried by illicit vendors, who
Soil the earth with their junked scraps....

And out of nowhere, a brigade of dogs
Casually stroll, sniffing the ground....
The dog feeder is around,
An aroma races ahead of her....
Bits of paper strewn,
Scoops of feed piled atop....
She moves on and the food
Disappears in minutes....
The papers blow away,
Adding to the litter....

Who cares?
Certainly not the daily sweeper....
Her broom swings with lethargy,
Gathering garbage into corners....
She is in an animated conversation,
Her cell phone moulded to her ear....
She doesn't care....
We watch....

* * * * *

## My Time....

When all is done
at the end of the day....
dishes washed....
family tucked in....
lights off,
I take a walk
around the house,
faintly illuminated
by the soft glow
of street lights.
I then say my prayer of thanks,
and stand alone
for a few moments
in the middle of our living room,
I feel a sense of sudden calm.
I'm alone....
just myself,
It is my 'me' time,
A short while,
but the best part of my day....
I guess we all need our space,
even....
if it is standing
for a brief moment
on an 18×18 inch floor tile.

* * * * *

## *The Long Walk Home.....*

A van stopped next to a tired man lumbering his feet on the hot gravel road. His oversized shoes were worn out and hampering his walk. A child, barely a year old, slept on one shoulder and a threadbare bag slung on the other. The woman next to him dragged her feet and tugged a sagging young child by the hand. They looked exhausted. An old lady and a man shuffled and staggered, moving unsteadily. The sun was playing cruel tricks, blazing relentlessly.

"Kahan ja rahe ho?" (Where are you going?) Asked the driver."Pata nahi," (Don't know) was the disinterested reply.

"Kabse chal rahe ho?"(Since when have you'll been walking?)
"Pata nahi" (Don't know)
"Kahan se ah rahe ho?" (Where are you coming from?)
"Pata nahi." (Don't know)

"I have space in my van," the driver continued speaking to the man in hindi, "I can give you and your family a lift. You all look so drained and fatigued. Let me help you all."

The tired man finally looked up and stared at the van driver for a long time. Surprisingly, there was a burning fire in his weak and weary eyes.

"We are six....we will fit but look at the back? Do you see the others....can you take them too?"

"No," said the driver, "that is not possible. Save yourself and your family. They too, will find a way to reach home."

The man sighed, leaning forward, peering at the sleepy and tired man behind the wheel. He had obviously been driving for hours.

"Sahib, you are a good man. You have actually stopped and offered help. We are invisible to most who travel these roads in comfort. But do you see these people behind us? Some of us started this journey together. Others we met on the way. We all have one goal. To reach home. We are each other's solace, comfort and support. If one goes, a limb has gone. We cannot lose hope. This fraternity keeps our faith alive. There is a reassurance in our togetherness. We are family. I do not abandon my family. We are in this fight together. You see this blood on the road? Soles are bleeding. Theirs, mine, ours! What does it matter, it is the same red! I say it again... we are family. We are fellow beings and all belong to this one great country. We do not see each other as 'migrants' but as brothers and sisters fighting a common war. If I leave them today, I will be a deserter. I cannot live with that stigma."
"But no one will know. They won't even notice your absence." The driver tried very hard to convince the man and his family.

"Yes, you are probably right, no one will realize we are not there. Look at them. They can barely see themselves. But sahib, I will know and that one truth will haunt me. My conscience cannot carry that burden."

The driver of the van was overwhelmed by the man's reply. Even in the face of such adversity, his conscience guided him. There is something greater than 'self'. There was such a humble honesty in that revelation and it taught him a heartfelt lesson that depressing afternoon, a lesson he never forgot.

"I am really speechless by your reply. You have so much honour, even in the face of hopelessness. But I wanted to give you a chance."

"Ahhh....honour is our garb, our blessing. It is our one possession no one can take away and it is not 'chance' that has put us on the road, my good man, but 'choice'. So I bid you farewell for now. You never know, we may just meet again one day. Now that would be 'chance'.

The van driver drove off. He had been given a valuable message that day. The men, women and children carried on their tedious trek. Some may reach home, some may not. But this time, the people who didn't have a voice took their destiny into their own hands. The rest was God's will.

Speak to me
Soul riders of a sundown beyond....
Serenades of a night breeze....
Qualms are many
And answers I seek....
Throw my way a shooting star....
So that I too may wish upon it....

* * * * *

## ***Lockdown......<br>Aftermath of a Migrants Journey Home.....***

Recently tarred,
To obliterate the old, injured roads,
But a solitary, subdued, muffled footprint
Remains conspicuous,
Is it a sole with a tiny hint of red?
Can you hear what it said?
I can....
The walker had once
Counted on utterances....
A cacophony of false promises,
Now jarring the senses....
Uttered with award-winning smiles,
And hands placed on their hearts,
In cunningness....
Oh, how they fabricated
To drown out the truth of
Temple bells, azaans, amens,
And every other prayer....
Do I see dark clouds,
Threatening a storm?
As an eerie sound,
Invisible cries
Of ghosts behind trees, wail,
Or is it hail,
Hitting us from the sky....

Did they get home?
Did we see a story?

Did anyone ask questions?
Just ragged pieces of soiled cloth,
Tattered pieces of discoloured strips,
Entangled in thorny bushes,
Spoke of someone who had 'passed'
This way....
Who were they?
The answer, yet again,
Smothered, snuffed out by
The blare of strident sounds,
On this spotless freeway,
Life goes on....

Once again....

The way beneath ponderous feet,
Smoggy air, heavy
With a hint of moonshine,
Head down, slow, cautious amble
On a potholed path,
Hurting with raw wounds,
They never heal....
Nor do the fragmented tracks,
That hide fallen red blooms
From a gulmohars tree,
Within their cracks....
Or is it a beaten path that bleeds?

*****

## ***The Song of Tomorrow.......***

The song has changed....
And the lyrics are whispering....
Your voice is my voice,
The words have a conviction of faith,
Riding on the wind,
The lilt of hope has angels wing
Courting a different wait....

An eagerness murmurs....
Takes my finger,
Leading me by my hand....
And says....
I have to leave behind
The yesterdays,
And understand,
That a tomorrow
Has come into view....

The song has changed,
And the sun shall rise,
As it did today,
And this is what it says....
That all is left behind,
It's now another day.

Listen carefully....
To a prophecy....
Bonding together....
We could be....
Once again....
One unfaltering chorus....
The song has changed....

*****

## *Just a Poem for Now.....*

Hear the winds of unfaltering feel,
Blowing through
With an elixir to heal,
That which has broken,
Fragmented in defeat,
Balm those soles
Of bleeding feet,
That have walked
This soil, as children of the earth,
And guardians in this place of rest....
Our ground of birth....

Hear that song that sings
To cull the hate,
Now in a loud hosanna
To dissipate,
Not with a crushing blow but
An anthem of love,
Riding in glory,
On the wings of a white dove.

Discard all who from rampart spew,
A venom of divide,
Then hide,
In the unholy creases of the
Of their own lies.

Lay your head
On each other's shoulders,

Seek comfort in knowing
You are there for each other and all,
And should you falter,
There are many a hand
That pick and cushion your fall,
For there is never such a thing as
A point of no return,
And there is no hell
Where you shall forever burn....
It's our world,
Our heaven on earth
So let us all live it.

Hear the winds of unfaltering feel,
Blowing through
With an elixir to heal
That which has broken,
Fragmented in defeat,
Balm those soles
Of bleeding feet,
That have walked
This soil, as children of the earth
And guardians in this place of rest....
Our ground of birth....

*****

## ***History.....***

So it shall be....
Of chronicled tales of history....
A past of war and blood and gore,
Wounds of old....festering evermore,
This pain shall ne'er cease to be,
Kept alive in history.

Seldom do chapters sing,
Praises in songs and hallelujah hymns....
'Tis the lust for power that's never gone,
In laments echoed in dirge and song,
Religion strokes on injured thrive,
By bias minds that keeps alive,
Peace cannot profit at length,
For those who prosper in a show of strength.

An argumentative mind loves a good fight,
Persistently debates realms of might,
So many a time, righteousness stands alone....
A great mind once wrote....
"The good is oft interred with their bones."

Look around today....is it not the same?
The beast still plays its devious game....
The good and fair are made to sleep,
Sealed lips suppressed to speak,

There are those who dare to hear,
Alas, they are deemed to live in fear....
So, can we, you and me,
Bid a final goodbye,
All that has gone, to let be,
Say, "Rest in peace, history...."

*****

## Migrants.......

Today I bumped into a friend. The last time I met her was a year before the covid lockdown had set in. We looked at each other, squinted, looked away, then looked again, and recognition dawned. Had we both changed so much in three years?

Both were wearing glasses. There was fatigue on her face.... must have been on mine too. We talked and caught up with this and that.

I came home and thought of those two years of the pandemic lost. All had changed.

We still had homes, but there were those who had lost everything. Those who left and walked till their soles' bled, are now returning to cities, once again, searching for jobs to feed families....bracing the cold and harsh weather.

What can I say....their 'lockdown' never ends....

They come in search of labour,
To soothe the burning ache of hunger....
Their night, a tree above and a wall for support....
Derelict, the home next door,
And a sadness in its story....
Aloof and unfriendly....

What dramas were played
Behind those wooden, locked doors?

Dimly visible through hazy morning lights,
The sun in furs, as the cold bites through smog,
The pulse of each breath,
Freezing in the mist of
A city's unforgiving winter....

Quiet, the feel of broken walls
And shutters down....
Unmoving in their defeat,
With the crushing of time gone by,
But still astir, in an abstraction
Of elapsed threads.....

Haunting nature of a silent street,
Lost in the back lanes of narrow labyrinth,
Enveloped intermittently by a stench of garbage,
And an aroma of deep-fried spices and steaming tea....
Here and there, the blackened ash of burnt twigs,
Smeared upon parts of broken tiles....
The fire was over long before night set in....
Yet there is a camaraderie
In a common discomfort,
Mute, but speaking about the
Desolation of ordinary, almost invisible things....

* * * * *

## ***Mundane...Yet, Not So......***

Have you ever, quietly, observed the scenes on pavements while being driven? They pass by quickly only because you are moving. Yet at times it gets you thinking, what are the narratives behind the sights you see. For, every picture tells a story......

Songs of the road....
Movements....in parts
And staying still at times....
All a part of a journey....
Pictures move....
A lonely, bent old lady walks wearily,
Burdened with a thought....
Will she be welcomed in her home?
Leafless trees, eerie gnarled branches,
Hauntingly etched across the sky....
An omen of times to come?
Temples and shrines bedecked along roadsides....
A silent prayer while passing....
A mere ritual or genuine belief?
Colourful street carts,
Enthusiastic hawkers shouting a sales pitch,
That is their lifeline....
Dreamers and doers,
A labourer with a silent gaze,
Does he have the luxury of thinking?
A lone dog, fiercely guarding his turf,
Daring any canine trespasser....
A young man with no legs,

Blessing all for alms....
Where does he get his strength to survive?
An empty bench....waiting....
Friends converse by a tea stall,
Re-kindling the lost art of talking....
Songs of the road....
Movements in parts
And staying still at times....
All a part of a journey....

*****

## ***Remember Me?***

Late night....
A city that seldom sleeps....
Gaps in a hurting wall, sitting idle,
Doorway to the rebirth
Of demolished hubs,
Once bearing old souls.

Stone pavements, washed of the day's dirt....
The night worker lays a 'table for two'
Under the sky of a watchful moon.

'Remember me?' Speaks an empty
Roadside stairway, leading nowhere,
Another time, another place....
In this big city of loneliness....

The way we are in this vast eternity
Of many happenings,
Just shadows of small things....
As we move,
Our footsteps vanish behind us....
We tread ahead,
Our imprints unknown....
'Tis the only way to go,
So we move on....

* * * * *

## ***The Importance of Being Who You Are......***

The importance of 'me'
Does not take you away to be
There for someone else....

The importance of 'me'
Is to write your name on your wall,
In a bright colour, so that other names by your side shine....

The importance of 'me'
Is to be able to dance with yourself,
Smiling at your partner from across the room....

The importance of 'me'
Is to buy flowers for yourself,
Because you are entitled to their fragrance....

The importance of 'me'
Is to be able to talk to yourself
For your heart listens to you....

The importance of 'me'
Is to accept the unacceptable,
Because you respect your strength....

The importance of 'me'
Is to hold your own hand in joy and sadness,
For that's the firm hand that guides others....

The importance of 'me'
Is to love yourself for who you are,
For you know that you can be tolerant of all....

* * * * *

## The Slow Climb.....

To stand atop of mountain high,
Closer to the sky,
Soaring into a successful vast,
Did I ever dream to getting there?

Nay....but, I did learn,
While I was beneath the soil,
Amidst rocks and trouble
I could never grow,
So I did pull out those roots....
Those ingrown shoots....
To another place way beneath....

Struggle to survive,
It taught this soul to rise,
Learning lessons from the wise,
"Now you can go no lower under,
So climb....climb,
It is only aloft, upwards, beyond...."
And so I stand
Atop a mountain high,
Closer to the sky,
Soaring into a successful vast,
Did I ever dream getting there?

*****

## ***Between Every Two Ways There is a Door……***

We pause between a moment before
And a moment after....
Fading colours turn into dreams,
The new bright, another voyage....
Once then....
Now ahead....
And following behind quietly
Is the sound of breathing,
In and out of a shadow of sequence....

Trapped in the night air,
Crowded with thoughts and
Fine mist from the light rain,
The soft tapping of drops
Is like a duet
Between conflicts or maybe acceptance....
I stand gazing at a light
Beaming from under
That door to happiness,
My eyes unblinking....
Hand on my heart....
Is it a door that I open to enter,
Or the one I closed?

Between every two ways
There is a door....

*****

## God's Children....

A certain group of people frequently feels marginalised in society. Because of the stigma attached to disabilities, families experience oppression, and disturbed and disabled children are kept inside their homes where they are denied equal access to jobs, education, and mobility.

Three young women....three different stories. All bound by one common factor. They live in a hutment colony close by. Their parents are either toiling day in and day out to make ends meet or, they live in fear of an inebriated father and brothers who would peddle anything to loiter aimlessly, dressed in so-called modern clothes, flashing mobiles and resorting to crime to fulfil their needs. These young women are mentally challenged or very disturbed. I have been seeing them for years. They appear in the vicinity, then disappear for months, or maybe years on end, then appear again. What is their life like? I don't know, but as I see threads weave together, I form a story in my mind.

Let's begin with Asha, the 'goat girl'.

My first encounter with her was an extremely dramatic one. Almost out of a thriller movie. I was at a friend's place, a building close to ours. We were enjoying a cup of coffee when we heard a lot of shouting and screaming outside. Opening the door in alarm, we saw a young girl, barely in her teens, cowering in a corner, next to the lift. She was petrified and I immediately noticed a large knife in her hand. The society watchman was standing on the staircase near our door, threatening her with a stick and all she kept yelling was "muje Jane do" (let me go). The rest was incoherent. Her clothes were dirty and threadbare and she did not look mentally stable. Through the closed wrought iron grill door, I asked the watchman what was happening and he explained very agitatedly that she lived in the 'basti'

(Hutment colony) next door. Some boys were chasing her. Lord knows how she got the knife but he saw her running into this building and chased her.

I heard her cry, "Didi muje bachao" (sister, please save me). She was shaking. She was scared and just a child. My friend and I told the watchman to go down and wait near the gate. We asked the girl to throw the knife down, towards us, get into the lift and go down. It took a long time convincing her, she was so scared. I quickly ran down the steps to ensure nobody harmed her, then walked her to the gate. The minute she was outside, she darted off at the speed of lightening.

A couple of years later, while walking my dog one evening, I heard a girl's voice call out. "Didi, didi, hello." It was the same young girl, a little older now, smiling and waving at me. I recognized her and waved back. She was gone in a jiffy. I saw she was neatly dressed but beyond that, I hardly got a glimpse. This time, no one was chasing her. She didn't look scared. Thereafter, I did catch a glimpse of her off and on. Many a time she would be walking with two, sometimes three, goats alongside. She always called out and waved. We had built a small rapport between us.

A few years later, we moved away but not too far from where we had lived for the past eight years. We got settled into our new surroundings. One day, looking out of our balcony, I saw a familiar sight....the young girl with her goats. Three of them. They walked by our building and then the goats got busy munching on the flowering shrubs I had planted outside our gate. “Hey,” I shouted, clapping my hand in irritation to draw attention. The ‘goat’ girl looked up startled but recognized me. “Hello didi,” she waved frantically. I smiled but told her to stop her goats from eating the plants. Realizing I stayed here now, she promised she would not spoil the plants. Then she asked about my dog. I was surprised she remembered. I would see her walking down our road quite often and was also happy to see her love for her animals. She had become a part of the small ‘regulars’ around our neighbourhood. A normal, mundane scene from an everyday street life.

One day, I asked my maid about her. I had seen them talking to each other, so she obviously knew her and curiosity got the better of me. I was told she lived with her mother and two older brothers. Her name was Asha. She was a normal child but fell very ill when she was about seven or eight years old. It affected her mind and she had been disturbed ever since. Because of her mental state, she was often teased and discriminated against by other kids and even seniors. At times, she would run away and then be found after a few days of searching, loitering or begging. Her family cared for her but she was not easy to handle as everyone worked and she was left alone at home. Seeing her love for animals, her brothers got her two goats. These pets were her saviours.

Looking after them, taking them on long walks, kept her calm and occupied. She never ran away again.

That was the story of Asha, the goat girl, when life had given her a respite and perhaps a bit of sanity and happiness.

Again, time passed. I forgot about her until one day, about five years later, my doorbell rang. There she stood....older, disheveled and very agitated. I was surprised and a bit disconcerted to see her like this. She kept asking for money. "Ten rupees, didi, ten rupees."

Something had gone wrong in these few last years that was obvious, so I gave her the money and she left. But that started it all.

Her visits didn't stop and the more I asked her to leave, the more aggressive she would become. It was becoming very uncomfortable and I could not handle the situation, so once again I asked my maid to take her home and explain to her family that if she kept coming and making a ruckus, the neighbours would report the matter to the police. After an angry tirade and a scuffle, she was taken away. I had to ask what had made her so disturbed. I was told that five years ago, her younger brother died drinking spurious liquor. The elder brother went away and her mother had fallen sick. One day, an elderly man came and took Asha away. He had paid the mother a hefty sum of money. This was another adverse side of humanity, the dark side. One can raise a voice and make noise about it but it exists and happens very often. Sometimes survival becomes an unjust masquerade. Six months later, the man brought her back. The traumas she must have gone through are silent. Yet all knew. No one did anything.

I had to go speak to her family and ask them to keep her away from entering our building. It was for her own safety. The mother nodded indifferently. Her brother, who had returned, promised she would not trouble us again. I remembered her goats. "Buy her a goat, it will keep her busy, looking after them like she did when she was younger." He told me the goats were stolen by boys and sold to the slaughterhouse. The same will happen again.

I haven't seen Asha since. Somehow, all learn to live through the underbelly of poverty that forces a human being into the darkest corners. But to fight through it with an unexplained strength, that is amazing. The will to survive is an undeniable fabric of every living being and these are God's children because they have no one else to protect them but an invisible hand that is guarding them.

The girl with a mobile phone is my next story.

I don't know her name but she is a regular in our tree lined avenue. Leaning against one of the parked cars, she is ever busy in an animated conversation that can go on for hours. A little theatrics gets thrown in while she is pacing. Dressed in jeans and a kurti, hair well-oiled and neatly tied, I never thought that anything was amiss. Though I would wonder how anyone could talk so much for hours on end, morning, noon and night. The amusing part was the emoting...anger, laughter, and serious concentration. Quite the actress.

Once again, Sunanda, my maid, filled me in one morning as I was watching her.

"Who is she and who does she talk to for hours on end?"

"She lives near our house," was the answer. "There is no one on the other end of the phone and this is what she does the whole day. She is also one of the few 'pagals'(mad) who live in our basti."

I hate that word 'pagal', but that was the easiest and shortest way people, known to her, would describe her state of mind.

"She is unaware of what is happening around her. Living in an imaginary world. Wouldn't we all like to be like that, unmindful of all the trials and tribulations and hardships," was Sunandas' distracted mumbling as she continued her mopping.

Amused, I observe her off and on. Quite apart yet a part of this world we live in.

I think to myself, occupied with analyzing the diverse roles destiny plays in keeping a variety of doors open. We are mere puppets, dealing with and getting past all the odds and ends thrown at us. Through her insanity, the 'mobile phone girl' had found her place of sanity and would probably go through life less troubled than all of us.

The Sujata story

A young girl in her twenties, hurriedly walking through lanes and by lanes of our secluded, picturesque colony. Her left shoulder and neck at a slight tilt to the left. A pretty face. Our neighbourhood is her beat. I pass her every evening on my walks. Brisk in her strides, she takes an occasional pause to look at her face in one of the side mirrors of any car or bike parked nearby. Out comes a lipstick. After colouring her lips a vermilion red, she admires herself, completely unaware of anyone passing by.

What is her story?

Sujata came to live in this vicinity as a child bride. She was barely a teen and was married off to a man much older. Her husband was an alcoholic and lame. He never worked. Child marriages are so common and the law often looks the other way. Seldom does anyone complain. It is a malaise in poor families, especially those who live in crime dominated areas. Gang wars, illicit liquor mafia dens and predators on the lookout for young girls to put into prostitution, force the parents to marry off their daughters before they fall prey to these sharks. Some find a happy home and some don't. That's their destiny.

Sujata was not lucky. While children her age studied and played, she toiled, cooked and worked. She was abused and brutally beaten by her husband, (a dirty, dark truth that also prevails in some of the most educated and affluent homes). As a result of a badly broken shoulder, she has an awkward tilt to her neck. After a few years of marriage, her husband suddenly died in a freak accident. Now it is just Sujata and her frail mother-in-law. A kind woman, often ill-treated by her son in the past, she has become weak and sickly.

Trauma leaves scars and mental scars become a life-long ailment. Sujata wasn't mentally challenged, but the years of abuse and domestic violence had taken a toll on her mind.

She now looks for whatever small jobs and errands she can get. Nothing permanent. I see her in and out of different bungalows and buildings, while I am on my evening walks, doing her rounds every day. She had approached me too but I had nothing to offer her.

Such are their lives. These are just three. There are many, many more. Victims of abuse, a little crazy and disturbed. There are shelters for these girls but one hears such horrific stories about these homes. It can be hell.

Something gives them the will to survive....

*****

## *The Story of Many a Shantabai.........*

She carries within the drapes
Of her folds,
Trysts of smouldering eyes
And stories untold,
Of quick intrigues,
A balm for the bruises
And a deep wound,
Covered by the arms of another.

Cowering alone in corners,
Shaken by a striking hand,
And ears ringing in an aftermath,
Of strewn tatters....
Ripped and torn,
In a wild array on the ground.

Her muffled screams and cries
From scrapes on the stony floor,
Barely shielded by the
Unhinged, cracked wooden door,
Merely raises a brow
Of every passer-by,
No one asks why....
It is the story of every Shantabai,
Who peers out of her little window....

Her forehead pressed against
The iron bars,
Creating a shadowed scar,

Lost in forbidden dreams....
But as she sees her reflection
Later in the day,
The dented shadow has gone,
Only to be replaced by another.

Waiting....waiting only for
The obscure of night,
In the know of raucous snores,
After violent fights....
And inebriation of broken glass....
Then slowly....with padded footsteps,
Down a dark alley,
Where her life begins,
Shrouded by the hours of darkness,
Only to end at sunrise once again.

*****

## ***The Falling Leaves......***

I have fallen
But not from grace,
The good earth is my place,
I have set myself free from
A bondage that held me high,
I now gradually fly....
Downwards to rest,
For I have risen to where I had to go,
Now in a slow,
An autumn leaf leaves its nest....

Through burning sun and heat,
Snow and sleet,
Winds and gales,
Thunder and storms,
I have held strong....
What finer medal
For serving a majestic tree,
Colour me gold....
Colour me bronze....
That is my award....
That is my reward....

* * * * *

## ***And Life Goes On....***

No, I don't long for my childhood,
(Well....maybe a little....)
It was a phase in mere passing,
That led on to my teenage years,
That too was not a lasting....

When that difficult line was crossed,
A step into the start of growing up,
'Twas not the toss of a little coin
That was to decide my future luck....

Now don't you be crying
For my adulthood,
That truly was my bane....
My choices were mine to make,
Though they did drive me insane.

Ahhh....then came the test,
For I had to share,
A piece of the pie, I had for so long,
But I did....with loving care....

Then came the pendulum....
Swing one side, then swing the other....
Responsibilities grew....
Sometime, I admit, I lay awake,
Wishing it was just me....or even two....

Don't feel sorry for yours truly,
That was my job, to be pulling my own hair....
The present seemed a jungle
My domain, in the lion's lair....

Oh no, I was not the king like him,
Maybe just a dithering prey....
Who had been thrown into tight spots,
Pull up your socks, I'd tell myself....
And be a soldier of the day....

The pulling and the pushing,
Bouncing up and down....
At times the nasty villain,
Then the jovial clown....

Yes....at times it was a battle,
And at times there was bliss,
And sometimes I'd ask for more,
Sometimes get more than my wish....

That phase has gone and well past,
It really wasn't that hard,
And now I love life and the way I played,
As fate dealt me its cards....

Each phase was a lesson,
That held me up strong,
How else would I know what to choose through these years,
'Tween what was right and what was wrong....

I did my turn, did I do alright?
Should get to know later, will have to wait a while,
To see how I am thought of,
When I look down at all and smile....

*****

## *Just a Fractured Window.......*

Forlorn broken window panes,
Hanging on splintered wood frames,
Held precariously by a rusted hinge,
Feathers from pigeon wings,
Trapped in jagged shards,
No one's looking in,
Or out....
All that remains is
Broken sunlight of half thoughts,
Going around in sad circles,
And the air heavy with a feel
Of lonely panoramas....
That era has long gone,
Shades of a lifetime,
Never to return....
So....

Who are you waiting for?
This 'once upon a home'....

*****

## Just.........

Just an accustomed, everyday street,
Out of nowhere....everywhere....
A lull of lethargy in the pace
Of a walking few and
Some scattered here and there,
Staring head down,
Or....
Into a faraway....
The old lady....flower seller....
Her face weathered, rough....
Not a face in the crowd, but
A crowd in her face,
Of having lived well beyond
Half a century of woes and cunning stealth....
To survive on these paths,
That is an art....

Looking around and above....
Side to side....
There is an inertia,
Yet everything is felt....
It is the 'everyday' of the same old,
Undiluted and unfiltered in its profoundness....
An average ambience of a place,
Hidden within the character

Of the same place....
Harmony in an old time of being
There forever....
Take it away and the vibes are gone,
And also a familiar flavour....

*****

## ***Dream, We Always Must....***

When we were young
We wanted to be so many things,
Touch the sky and fly with wings,
Nothing seemed impossible....

We had the daring and guts to try,
We would laugh at fun,
And at the drop of a hat, cry,
Emotions were never pent-up....

Then we grew a little more,
Life seemed somewhat
Harder than before,
Though we still dreamed,
But there were slight hurdles
In our minds,
And sometimes the path
Was a little confusing to find,
But we sailed through....

We took risks, we took many a chance,
We partied, we danced,
The shoulder never really carried any weight,
Took whatever was served on our plate,
Fell in love....broke hearts,
Left the negatives behind,
Made new starts,
The problems were solvable....

Then we really started to grow,
The world began its reality show,
It was okay to dream, but real life,
It was a different cup of tea,
Suddenly, we were not so free,
Commitments, priorities
Had raised their heads....

Now we had taken on a different role,
Sometimes dying to be reckless and bold,
But a hand held us back,
Maturity had set in,
It wasn't always a win, win,
Adulthood was another game....

But hey.... you can never say,
Childhood motivations have a way,
Of finding that pursuit
When there was a thrill,
Where there is a way, there is a will,
And not give up because the goings are rough,
It may be very tough,
Yet dream, we always must....

*****

## *Ordinary is So Special.......*

I am sixty-nine plus and getting on....
And I love to look at the sky....
The birds, the clouds, the sunset....
I love the way the trees grow....
Shed leaves and regrow....
I love watching nesting bulbuls, crows,
And munias, who make my balcony
Their home every year....
I love the fragrance of the raat-ki-rani,
The rangoon creeper flowers
And the frangipani....
I love to gather fallen flowers....

I watch the daily pace of women and men
Who walk the road in front of my home,
Going to work every day....
They have a purpose, a determination,
To give their family and children a better future....
That, to me, is so inspiring and meaningful....
They struggle, have a hard life,
But always smile....
To me, that is saying, "Thank you, God, for this gift called life."

I love watching stray dogs
Chase each other....play and roll,
Then wait diligently for the good people
Who come every evening to feed them....
They, to me, are apostles of God,

Selfless in their serving....
I love to watch wasps, butterflies and bees....
Flirting, busy, undistracted in their quest....
They are the saviours of our earth....
Without them and other small beings
Nature will die and so will we....

I love the cacophony of traffic, sometimes,
I love the silence of the night....
It reminds me yet again
That we live on this earth with everyone, everything,
But have sadly stopped respecting it....
I love to look down when I walk....
Many times, to make sure I do not trip,
But also to tell myself, this ground is yours....
Keep your feet on it....

*****

## Story of an Empty Chair.....

Portrait of a lone chair,
Resting on an uneven concrete floor,
Of a bare terrace….
Its seat threadbare and worn,
Maturing in a quiet, undisturbed way,
Bearing the brunt of hidden stories
And the weight of ageing limbs
For many years....
Now, it sits staring into loneliness....

For perching crows and sparrows
A respite now and then....
And no one else....
Untill a gust of wind blows
And aching joints creak in a hush
'Missing you'....

*****

## *On the Other Side, We Shall Meet....*

We shall meet there again
On the other side of silence....
Where voices went beyond
And between tangled wires
And old bricks....
Where senses soaked
In the unspoiled
Hues and tones of raw
Feelings, spiced in
The piquant morsels
Of nostalgia.
And then shall we reminisce
Images of our past....
Some spoken....
Some wrapped in
The wordless warmth
Of thoughts....
We shall raise our cups
In salutation....
When we meet there again,
On the other side of silence....

*****

## ***Empty Shoes........***

Silent steps,
Empty shoes by the door,
Waiting....waiting....waiting....

Survival in another form,
A tangible pattern of cobwebs,
Entwined with the sole....
A woven tapestry of time....

This is now,
That was then,
New challenges....
One life....one fate....

Silent steps,
Empty shoes by the door,
Waiting....waiting....waiting....

*****

## ***Ode to a Woman........***

Woman....
Your beauty shines,
Not for others to appraise,
But for you to stand out....

It is not the way that you look,
But the strength of your features....
It is not the way that you dress,
But the power in your poise....
It is not the silver in your hair,
But the wealth that you wear....
It is not the creases on your brow,
But the integrity of your thoughts....
It is not the stoop of your shoulders,
But the toughness of your ability....

Woman....
Your allure and grace radiate,
You do not eclipse others,
Your being there inspires....

*****

## Listen to Your Soul.......

I have seen myself grow....
It has been a journey long,
Yet every stage brought something new,
Youth was an endless song....

I have come a long way,
And so have you....
At times, the path was tough,
Yet, now here I am
Through it all,
The gentle and the rough....

I can feel the change....
My body has taken on another style,
The grey streaks, softly relaxed waist,
Been there for quite a while....

I ache a lot more,
My skin may have lost its glow,
Back is not so supple, joints do pain,
Patience does a longer dance,
And tolerance a little slow....

In all this, as I reflect,
My thoughts, now, are so much there,
In the wisdom of loving smaller things,
And the depth of how I care....

Time has taught me wisdom,
To hear more than to speak,
And follies were actual lessons,
That coached me how to teach....

For every little detail in colour,
People and a new praise,
For so much all around,
To respect all that I have gained,
It's a new life that I have now found....

*****

## ***That One Lonely Moment.......***

He stares at the night sky,
A dark without the moon,
The need to go somewhere....
Anywhere....maybe reach up
And talk to that one lone star....

Unfolds his wooden ladder
To exit through a boarded window....
That too was closed forever....
Slats distressed and bound by rusted nails,
A niche in the wall of utmost sadness,
He had nowhere to go....
Even though there were no barriers,
The space was open wide and free....
But he felt the walls....

The rooftop silent while all sleep,
He sits and waits for dawn....
Ambling amid many a silence,
Through his overcast thoughts....
A poem of breaking sunlight....
Falls upon dried leaves
And crawling ants....
Some still live outside their home....
Then it starts to rain....
Or,
Was he crying for just being
An unknown face in the crowd....

*****

## *Much More.....*

You are not
What you want others to think....
You are not
What you think you should be....
You are not
About wondering, 'did I get it right'....
You are not
To wait for the world to reveal your worth....
You are not
A thought....a 'next time' a 'not now'....
You are more.....
You are much....much more....

Moving peacefully
Towards the sunset,
My eternal present
Is always seeking inspirations
Between the old world
And new mystical moments....
Fine wrinkles on my face
Highlight the radiance
Of my eyes as I look into
Images of my life thus far....
Ageing gracefully is not fading,
It is a challenge......
A conversation with
Unexplored chapters begin....
Between waking and sleeping,
We embrace the next....

If there is music,
Let it not be muted,
The art of existence is
Not in losing oneself,
But creating new canvases....
Do not let anyone make you disappear.

*****

## *A Page in the Life of a Human Being....*

A hutment colony, shanty shops, litter-strewn corners, and stray dogs tearing apart packages in search of food, congest the lane. Horns honking and a general pandemonium made me feel that I was taking part in an obstacle race. I passed by a man sitting on a shabby, weathered, wooden bench. His clothes were threadbare, unkempt hair and bare feet. I had seen him a few times whenever I walked down this road. Today I noticed he was reading a yellowed, slightly crumpled newspaper. I paused....he seemed engrossed.

'He is educated, yet.....,' I said to myself, for that sight I saw spoke a lot in unsaid words. Sadly, I wondered what his story was.

My mind dwelled on him for a long time after....his life.... his hopes. How did he reach this roadside destination?

Shackled to a bench by the roadside,
By habit....
Cracked soles of numbed feet,
Hand carelessly turning pages
Of bygone news, printed on crackling
Soiled paper....
That is all he can afford....but
He can read....
That says a lot, amid
Smoggy soot and smell
Of coughing rickshaws,
Dragging threadbare tires

On ailing roads,
Potholed by the disease of urban apathy....
Bruised doors of his mind and soul,
Coming face to face
With hope....
A small leaf struggling,
Not unlike himself....
Seeds blown by the wind....
Finding a meaning in life....
Searching for lost soil and time
Somewhere....
A portrait through cracks
Of a battered footpath....
Dried stem of a tulsi,
Trying to find a light
That might not last....

He sleeps in his silent
Sense of a lost space,
As dusk exhausts....
Covered by the remains of the day,
Blown away by a tepid night breeze,
Only to wake to a 'mourning' dawn
Of a merciless world,
Looking once again for happy colours....
Maybe life will shine, catching a glimpse,
Looking out through a hole in the torn
Old paper of forgotten news....
Life goes on....

*****

## ***Sometimes.....***

Just quietness....
Cushioned back....
Warm feet....
A mild fragrance in the air....
Sometimes....
Just stillness....
Clouds....birds gliding....
A window to stare....

Sometimes....
Calm brows....
Just no thoughts....
Nowhere to go....
Sometimes....
Time standing still....
Hearing my own heartbeat....
My breath in slow....

Sometimes......

* * * * *

## ***Our Moments to Shine...***

When we talk about our dreams,
There is always sunlight in our eyes....
We are the strongest,
When we have nothing to lose....

This moment you live,
Is your wealth....
Choose who you share your time with,
Entrust with care....
It will not return....

Not all things that break make a sound....
And not all broken pieces are visible....
And inside a noise there may be a song,
Handle feelings with compassion....

We all have our moments to shine....
Let it be just ours and not an image
Of someone else....

*****

## *A Mother Was Once a Child......*

She was a young girl,
Hair flying wild,
Features mild....
A dance in her steps,
Mischief in her eyes,
Day-dreaming and carefree,
Her eyes saw much more
Than they could see....
She felt she owned the world.

As she grew,
Dreams became a few,
The wildness tamed,
But music still made her dance,
She took a romantic chance,
And waltzed into a new life....

The years went by....
Some dreams still made her smile,
Her thoughts wandered,
But just for a while....
Songs were tapering in her head,
The chores of living had slowed
Her down to home and stead,

Her sway was slow
As was her spark....
And often did she gaze at her reflection,
After dark,

When no one saw her....
With a tired head down,
Looking at those worn hands
And fatigued feet on the ground,

Soon the time came
And her nest felt forlorn,
Children gone....she sat alone,
Trying to recognize an image
Of a wide waist and silver hair,
Her face lined with all stories
Of the past,
Her aching joints and tedious walk,
But of a life well borne....

For now, she has passed on
Her youthful dance and song,
To those who had loved her spirit wild,
Now cushioned in her ample arms
As a child....
Yet....
She would never know,
But those who were nurtured
By her wealth of giving and
Of just being always there....
A lifetime of silent love and care,
She was beautiful forever....

* * * * *

## *And I Thought......*

And then I thought,
There by the sea,
The sand....smell of
Salty tides, making memories....
We didn't come here by choice,
But here we are,
Making things work....
Growing with each journey,
Each landmark,
Every mood....emotion....
Believing in things others do not....
Navigating our spirits through
Laughter....sadness,
Light and dark,
Loving and living,
Knowing where you were,
And have come to be,
As your own unique self....
And see where it takes you....

We are here only for a while,
Be your own home....
Reach out for what you want
And it will reach out to you....
Moving on....challenging yourself....
Stirring that belief....

Feeling the magic at times....
Let it break, mend and move on....
Sunset to sunrise....
Grow old slowly....
The best is yet to come,
Always....

*****

## *Destiny.....*

There I poised by the closed door,
Hearing whispers on the other side,
Was it my past telling me stories,
Or my future in hide....
Dare I open....
And dwell on what has passed,
Or....
See a panorama of a life to come....
'Tis then I ask....
If I knew what was to be,
Would I have taken
This journey at all....
How would I have learned
Each time I rose after a fall?
The need to learn will never exist,
If everything that was, is to be,
Let whispers remain behind those doors,
As my destiny....

*****

## *A Canvas of Little Big Things in Life....*

I picked up a pebble from here
And a stone from there....
Gently held a fleeing feather
In the air....

Petals shed, strewn on the ground,
I gathered each one lying around....
'Tis then I add a stolen bliss,
Stirring a dream and a wish....

A melody of bird songs....
A flicker of sunlight,
Borrowed moonbeams from the night....
Laughter of joy....also
A hint of tears....
Burst of confidence mingled
With a little fear....

A hug from loved ones,
Embrace from a friend....
Even a little anger....
Then pieces of wood,
For a bridge I wanted to mend....

Wag of a tail, a breath....a sigh....
That chipped wooden box
Of childhood memories....
Tugged at heartstrings or made you cry....

A stranger's wave of hand,
A shoulder and a smile....
Paint all these little big things together....
It makes it all worthwhile....

* * * * *

## ***Tread With Care....***

Tread with care....
Speak with thought....
The truth is out there,
It is brittle....delicate....breakable,
Like eggshells....
Graze not the wound....
It is still raw underneath....
And the tenderness
Still aches....
Tread with care....
Speak with thought....
The truth is out there,
It is brittle....delicate....breakable,
Like eggshells....

Use each step to take you forward,
Let the journey reach its course,
Come not on the way of another,
Should you falter
The other will fall too....
It is then the journey
Becomes a hindrance
And neither shall move ahead....

Tread with care....
Speak with thought....
The truth is out there,
It is brittle....delicate....breakable,
Like eggshells....

*****

## ***Be Not My Judge....***

Who am I to judge you
Or anyone....
Just as you cannot know me
Without bearing my pain,
My happiness, sins, my loss and gains....
So, it is also with you....
Only I can look back and judge myself,
That is in my power....
Call it a privilege or torment....
But what lies ahead....
I will not know till my last breath....
I call it my blessing....

*****

## *Dear Door……*

Between a step outside and one within
The space seemed so wide….
Many voices, manipulative actions
And consequences wait in hide.
I entered a door, leaving myself outside,
Who walked in?
I don't know….

* * * * *

## ***Conversations With God.....***

God asked man....
"Why do you keep me away, locked
Behind doors and
Incarcerated within concrete walls?
How can I reach you?
Keep me close in your heart."
Man looked perplexed....
"Heart....what's that?"
God smiled...."When I made you,
I put in a heart
To live within you....
It makes you feel,
Gives you emotion,
Guides you....
Gives you life."
Man laughed, intoxicated with power,
"You are mistaken, dear lord....
I made you....made myself....
Made the world and
I will decide who shall live in it
And who shall die!"
God went silent....
Then he whispered....
"Reach out to me when you need me....
I am always there for all....
But first, set me free,
Only then shall you hear me."

*****

## *Creation......*

What is being....creation....
Breath....existence?
What is life?
Life is the weight you carry....
It is the legacy you bear....
Life is the heritage handed down to you....
Life is substance....
The fabric, the birth, roots, survival, the demise....
Life is the ancestry, the traditions, values, the morality,

Convictions and teachings,
Life is given to us....

'They were....therefore, we are....'

The potential handed down to you
May just adorn
The palm of your hands
In a small amount,
Or....
Enfold your being in opulence....
It is the weight you carry....
The legacy you bear....
A heritage handed down to you....
It is how you choose
To take it forward....

Life is substance....
Whatever your destiny,
Honour it as a tribute,
To those guardians before you....

*****

## We Are Just Stories....

We were all born one day....
And we shall go....
We are all stories....
Be courageous when telling your story
The way it is....
It will free you....
For life is scarred....
But beautiful too,
If you let it be....

This infinite existence is just a show,
There is so much yet to know....
And we really should never let it slip away,
For, habitually, the sun sets to lose the day,
The moon disappears in light,
It has to part with the night....
But it is an illusion....
It is not gone....
Make your life a journey
Much like the sun, the moon....
They set only to rise again....
Shining through clouds....after rain....

*****

## *To Heal......*

To heal
You have to hurt,
To understand the power of happiness,
You have to know the debility of sadness,
To value the weight of respect,
You have to go through humiliation,
To love unconditionally,
You have to experience rejection,
To give with your heart and soul,
You need to carry the agony of
Being denied,
To relish peace and
Realize the importance of the moment
You are living in right now, you need to encounter
The fatigue and loss of what has passed.

*****

## ***Poverty Along the Footpaths.....***

Our car stopped at a red light. There was a traffic jam. On my left was a flyover and under it, a few destitute, poverty-stricken people, sat huddled. They were immobile and sat like the dead. One slept or was intoxicated? One was missing legs, the other, missing an arm. They were not there yesterday. There were some rags and bundles scattered around, along with plastic bags. I stared and stared. The cars were not moving. How do they survive? Where does the will to live come from? But I guess they too love their lives as we all do. I felt very heavy....went home and penned these words. That day, the image didn't leave me. There are so many like them all over every city, yet we merely glance at them as we pass by. Have we become numb to humanitarian tragedies?

Sometimes sad roads sing a serenade
To all the homeless....
The screeching tyres and wheezing engines
Acts as a cradle song....
A hooting owl screeches a lullaby....
A comfort level
For the unhoused, living rough
In their familiar surroundings,
'Tis the only home they know....

Huts along the footpath....
For some, just a dirt ground....
A bare string tied to two poles
And ragged laundry of the living

Billows....
The only sign of activity
Among a derelict world
Of dirt-smeared faces
And broken eyes that say," Bury me here...."
In this loneliness of graveyards,
Alms come into a dented pan,
Dropping slow....
A path on the side,
Lost to broken tiles and weeds,
Leading to a forgotten past....
Stained wall with shreds of red,

Uncut, dry plants....
And a niche....cobwebbed....
No one has a home
In this, an uncertain world....
A stained hand clasps a consoling
Cup....is it tea?
Life goes on
In this canvas of an endless city....
For those who couldn't survive,
The day ends in this city of bare trees
With amputated limbs and missing portraits....
Others sleeping between two graves....
One where dreams died....
The other, where all hopes were laid to rest....
And caged birds don't sing....

*****

## ***Took My Breath Away......***

Amidst all that quietness
I was not alone,
A gentle breeze touched me....
And then I saw beauty....
It was fragile, but not broken,
And it danced,
Not because it moved,
Or there was music,
But because
The world continued to turn....
Only for a moment
Did time stand still,
For it was then, it took my breath away....

A quiet anticipation
Of happier times,
Two friends talk in silence....
And in that space of the unsaid,
Brief passing moments
That slip by unperceived,
Quietness becomes tangible,
And thoughts are touched....

That feeling....
That time is passing
Infects your need to hold on,
And the sadness with time passing,
Some things cannot stay....
We move towards a sunset,

Echoing through dim lights....
A finale of each day,
And the beginning of another....

So still and deep
Is this space inside
That never grows old....
'Tis only the noise of the outside
That ages all....

* * * * *

## ***The Slum-Dweller and His Neighbour......***

All his precious possessions
In a sack, clenched by a fist,
His home....a door hangs by a rusted hinge,
Creaking in pain....
Concealed behind a threadbare drape,
Faded by an onslaught of sunlight,
Torn, the jagged edge,
Entwined into twisted nails,
And a window with no face....
Just broken bars and glass panes,
Staring into a yawn of darkness,
Sometimes the light warily creeps in....

In this world of so much and more
"What do you own?" I asked him....
"Just what the weight of what one hand can carry,
I need the other to provide for my existence."

In this world of towering high rises
And sprawling homes
"Where do you live?"
"A place where I can sleep,
A door to enter,
And a window for air.....
For the rest of the day
I need to be in the open,
So my eyes can look up at the sky
To pray and dream while I am awake."

Who are you?
"I am who many do not want to be,
Yet I do not want to be them either,
I walk my own way,
Because for now I am free...."

*****

## ***The Forgotten Grave......***

Curtains lightly drawn, letting in
Serene music of fading summer lights....
A soft beam gently lays its hand
On a portrait, frozen in time....
The vintage paper with creases and
Torn corners do not fade her beauty....
Where does she dwell now?
Perhaps only in memories,
A large, silent space of remembrances
Wordless, quiet, yet so alive,
In a mind where everything happens,
Yet invisible......

I lie beneath dried leaves and discarded stones....
Wild bushes grow as a prayer....
The mulberry tree over my grave
Gives but slight shade
From the scorching sun,
That has bleached my tomb
Erased my name....
For who am I?
Just someone who walked
With you,
At times, uneasy in the summer light,

Many a path into the night,
Each one....together, yet apart,
Journeying this land briefly....
Nothing was happening....

Yet everything was happening,
As thoughts met....a mental portrait,
Then forgotten....
Once upon a time....
Till we meet again....
For now....resting....
In the middle of everywhere....

*****

## The Tree......

There stood a tree, rooted tall,
No storm or gale could make it fall,
Winds shook its leaves when autumn came,
Come spring, the splendour was the same....
Rain watered and the earth gave feed,
The majestic tree gave back in need,
It gave fruits and provided shade,
Within its cover, many homes were made,
Seasons came and years went,
The anchored tree had spent
A lifetime nurturing all,
It let no resides ever fall....
Then came a weed, small in size,
Dipped in poison because it could not rise,
To the stature of this grand sentinel in wood,
It hated the ground where the tree stood,
Full of hate, like a toxin it tried to spread,
Thinking it would create a dread,
And all the denizens would eventually flee,
Alone would stand, this imposing tree.

The poison of hate kills the mind,
For malice towards another will never find,
A place to grow if the heart is true,
Those who despise, shrink to a few,

The venomous weed wilted, devoured by its own deeds,
Victorious stands the righteous tree,
For strength lies in one's belief that shall not sway,
By seeds of contempt that come their way.

*****

## ***Do Not Go Beyond....***

Do not wander beyond....
Lest you stray or get forgotten,
For let your feet walk thus far,
But do not get lost....
Hold not too much,
For limbs cannot carry
More than they need....
Beyond an embrace,
It overflows to waste....
Find within what you have,
And expand to where you can reach,
Pursue no more....
Make that your world,
And you shall have enough....

*****

## *An Elusive Moment of Creativity.....*

I started writing this poem early morning today. What inspired me to write it? I have no idea. Sometimes I get lost in the words, so I reread to figure out what was going through my head as I wrote the lines.

Discover your own thoughts within these words.

My inner awareness is my secret....
Is your secret....
This silence is no better place....
Within a space....
The wanderings between
Mind and soul
And the inner being
Is like an eternity....infinity,
Absorbing....
Enlightening....
We meander through many
A scar of night and day,
For nothing dies....
That does not live....
So soul....be good
Lead us home....
Sometimes I go half-crazy
At the wonder of excitement
In small things....
Not on all days,
But some days....
When I think,

The pink
On the palette is just right....
Because the red in the
Gulmohar tree is about to bloom....
And the raucous Koels are celebrating,
The pale purple, lilac Jacaranda, blossom
Outside my window....
And it is not too late to experiment
With just that one fanciful thought,
Of creating something out of nothing….
And I did it,
Because no one was looking anyway....
At the moment, I am in that
Delightful frame of mind,
It is like a body song....

Within words there is poetry,
I listen more than I speak,
And everything seems alive....

For nothing dies....
That does not live....
So soul....be good
Lead us home....

*****

## ***Too Brief.....The Season......***

The morn has toned down
To an end of a day....
I lay under the stars,
Uniting with the soil and my breath....
For that moment, I disappear
Into the wide open space above me,
Awed by a canopy of adornment....
The full moon keeps me company
Playing games....
'Now you see me,
Now you don't,'
I play along....
Humming an old favourite song,
"Fly me to the moon...."
A tepid breeze drops a leaf on my face,
One, two, then an agitation of many....
No, autumn is a while away....
It's a letter from the tree....
"Don't cut me," it torments....
"I gavc you lifc...."
"Hoot," speaks the owl,
"Save my home,"
I can hear the forest spirits whisper....
Their muted cry haunts me....
Just then, clouds swallow the moonlight
And all becomes invisible,
The sky, in a brief message,

Abandons all for just a while,
Forecasts in hushed tones....
"If you cease to hear....

I shall cease to be"
Something told me the truth
That night, as I felt the leaf
On my face....
I realized, seen from another world,
We are but a dabble....a speck,
But deem ourselves greater
Than that glorious moon....
How disdainful are we in our foolishness....
It is summer and I lay long into the night,

Until the stars crossed over....

*****

## *Yin and Yang......*

Inside happiness, there is sadness,
In a good, there is also a bad,
Within courage, there is a hint of cowardice,
Along with joy comes tragedy,
Generosity, also carries with it greed,
Humility can hide arrogance,
And at times, peace camouflages hostility,
Dark clouds can flood or quench thirst,
As a fire can burn or illume,
There is black,
There is white,
There is a day,
There is a night,
There is weak,
There is strong,
There is right,
There is wrong,
Life is a walk on a tightrope....
And the edge is so very close....
Balance is pivotal....

*****

## *Old World....*

Faded, rusted, time-worn,
Patina coated, tattered, torn,
Dented artifacts
Do not need to be thrown....
No....they need to be valued more,
You need to own
Their tone, character,
Emanating a distressed radiance....
Look closely....
The wear and tear embraces
A history....chronicle, a memoir,
A diary of how life plays out....
Neglect seldom shouts....
But read the stories....
They speak through layers of tarnish, treasure them....
Ageing gracefully is the attraction,
A validation of a life well lived,
These vivid pieces speak
More than is said....

*****

## *Dance of the Looms......*

Dance, my friend, dance....
Dance like coloured threads in the breeze,
And weave a tapestry of unspoken words
That are free....free....
Imagination cannot be knotted in captivity,
Hues of emotions, crazy shades of real,
Entwined in a pattern, then worn,
Medley of mixed....
Fusion or torn....
Who cares....blown away....
A few threads here, there....
Covered in drapes,
Then bare....
Dance, my friend, dance.....
Dance like coloured threads in the breeze,
And weave a tapestry of unspoken words
That are free.....free....
Imagination cannot be knotted in captivity....

*****

## ***The Wonder of Being Alive.....***

The wonder of being alive
In this world, where
Chaos reigns outside my window,
And somehow the day
Seems to have been taken over
By hostile voices....

I feel alienated....I feel vulnerable....
Wrapping my arms tightly around
Myself....
Shielding those I love within my heart....
I feel defenseless.....
The blue sky and the free birds
Are writing an ominous story
With the clouds....

Nightfall comes....I am restless....
As I tip toe back and forth,
With a platter of leftover crumbs
And a few morsels....
Sitting cross-legged among crumpled sheets,

Staring at the full moon
Casting shadows, I enjoy the sound of
An odd rattle passing by....probably
A late night shift....
My fingers rummage, picking tidbits
From my plate, I nibble absent mindedly,
Licking my fingertips,

Savouring the trace,
Every tinge of flavour....

This feel of a bite in my mouth
Never tasted better than now,
The piquancy remained....not too obvious,
But like intangible remnants
Of fine dust....
Now the night on the outside seems different,
Not too threatening,
The dark, with its odd hooting,
A lone dog barking,

Feels like the world I want to live in....
A smile as I recollect a bit of this,
A bit of that....
I take another adventurous bite....
It tastes far nicer than the over salted
Dish I had made a few hours ago....
I hear soft whispers...mellow giggles,
As a couple walk past....
A late night tryst perhaps?

I feel secure....
On familiar grounds of a small world,
Just around me....
Humdrum....
Ordinary suddenly matters more....
More precious....irreplaceable....

I realize....I cannot lose these moments,
These every-day, truthful moments....

I smile yet again and hug myself,
The wonder of being alive....
Take another chew and magically
The salty, slightly burnt morsel
Is the tastiest bite I have ever had....
Then I hum an old song befitting
My existing comfort zone....
"......and I think to myself, what a wonderful world...."

*****

## ***The Cage....***

That little bird flew away....
Leaving an emptiness imprisoned
Within its cage....
Woeful is that solitude,
And mute is the silence
That echoes in that place....
An emptiness is always
Full of explicit sentiments....

The prison doors are open....
The cage door ajar....
The ensnared are out....
The locked are unbound....
The detained are let loose....
Yet...
That space....
That space where a captive is confined,
Still has a feel of bondage....
It never feels empty....
There is a story that lingers....
There is a tale that haunts.
An unlocked cage is never free....

*****

## ***Way Out....***

Being positive is like
Clasping a lit candle....
It will guide a way out....
And all the darkness that surrounds you
Shall also find an outward path....
For even darkness
Needs a light to find an exit.

*****

## ***Wars......***

Of wars....what can I speak,
Of those who bleed....
From their soul,
From their heart,
From their wounds,
Of wars, they want no part to be....

Beauty burned to rubble, razed,
Limbs shattered....eyes glazed,
Soldiers march....guns in hand,
Unreal....your land....my land....

What does it matter to those graves,
They are gone....you say they were brave,
But nay….
Their hearts had fright and many
tears,
Their hands and bodies shook with fear,
Now look around....for all that is gone,
Did it matter to those buried underground?

Of wars....what can I speak,
Of those who bleed,
From their soul,
From their heart,
From their wounds,
Of wars, they want no part to be....

*****

## ***We Are.......***

We are....
The choices we make,
The risks we take,
The weak and the rough,
The unbroken, the tough,

Sometimes....
Reaching for the stars,
Or feet on the ground,
Docility in silence,
Rebellion in sound,

We might....
Have lost a lot,
Or gained much more,
Opened a way out,
Yet closed some doors,

Laughed a lot,
Also shed many tears,
Faced the hard with courage,
Or pulled back in fear,

Yet here I am,
And here you are,
Wading the shallows,
Swimming the deep,
As Robert Frost said...
I quote, "Miles to go before I sleep...."

*****

## *Open Windows......*

Some captivating moment....
Some reflective musings....
As my eyes reach up to a sky,
Lit up by a high rise,
Leaning against a night,
Housing people whom I have never met....
A lull in the quietness of a sunset.

A gentle breeze wafting across my face,
I look ahead and read into
A theatre of everyday normal....
Yet, as I gaze upon open windows,
Lucent in a golden glow within,
Each window outlines a saga
Of small peaceful or
Another mundane day....
Some toils, some tribulations at play....
I ponder, eyes closed in fleeting,
And many a story stage in my head,
As I recline on an easy chair,
Clicking pictures inside my mind....

There is joy in one square of glass pane,
Laughter ringing loud....
Elation of a big gain?
Then perhaps hope in another,
Coping with forgotten illusions....
A cry of grief and tears....
Subdued aura of loneliness

In missing someone....somewhere,
Wistful stares
Into nothingness,
Could be silent sadness,

Behind that curtain,
As it waves in a subtle blow,
I catch a glimpse
Of a figure lost in thoughts....
Maybe a broken dream
Of wants that were not to be....
Emotions on display, a drama,
Making its debut in many acts till
The curtains come down....

A kaleidoscope of glimpses
Of a journey taken by us all....
It can be you....me
Or,
Any one of them....
In rehearsal or reality....
We are all just one of the same
In it together....
And I realize as I walk in and
Close my doors,
We are all bound collectively
In this humanness of being united,
As each one has
A bit of our story in them....

*****

## ***The Weight....***

When autumn turns
And the foliage....
Ah, they too shall fall....
And trees will look
Like the green woods have passed away....
But nay….
It is not so....
You and I know,
When all leaves fall,
The forest has not demised....
Spring shall come again....

Life again shall rise….

And so be it for those,
Who carry the onus
Of a leaden past,
The burden shall not last....
For....
That too can be shed,
Laid on an undisturbed ground,
All that is borne, tires one's back.
It can be eased....
A carried weight
May always be put down....

*****

## ***Harmony.....What Lies Within***

What I seek,
I hold in my hand....
Within, it is unbreakable....
It is precious....unthreatened....
I choose the freedom
To keep it hidden....
Undisturbed....
Unsullied by opinions....
Smiling on the inside....
I find it beautiful......
Harmony....

What I seek inwards,
I am aware....
In between somewhere....everywhere....
Invisible....yet it is there....inside....
Significant in its anonymity....
Unknown to most....
Unseen by judging eyes....
It is beautiful in its insignificance,
Because it has not been exploited....

* * * * *

## ***Keep Going.....***

When a thunder storm rages
And the wind, rain blur your path....
Don't turn back....
Take shelter....
The storm shall pass....
The way will clear....
And the sun will come out....
Keep going....

Continue to walk with your head high,
Move your pace with time....
For a stationary dot is insignificant,
Unless drawn into a moving line....
Be it any shape or length,
To reach an end, you have to start....
A line is a picture of design,
That makes every journey a work of art....

* * * * *

## *A Kind of Apathy Has Set In...*

I took a drive down the
Busy roads,
Sandwiched between
Parked cars and two-wheelers,
A haphazard array,
In-between, a profusion of people....
Aimless, masked and unrecognizable....
Happy being inconspicuous....
Walking....window shopping....
Tripping on disgruntled tiles
Of broken footpaths....
Amidst scaffolding still there
From last year, or was it before that?
Waiting for cans of paint to emerge
From neglect, just lying on the side....
Shutters down....
Tells a story of bleeding hearts
And a deep sadness,
For those who have gone
Either which way....never to return....

How I would enjoy a stroll....
That seemed not so long ago....
Browsing and enjoying knick-knacks,
Cheekily bargain hunting
And returning thrilled with bags
Of not so necessary things
But enjoyment.
Now the unease is palpable....

Hesitatingly, do I venture out,
Just to feel a sense of relief
When I return,
Within the safety of my four walls.
Is it only me....I wonder....

Trenches dug up everywhere....
Mounds of dirt
Have made a permanent home....
I get reminded of a graveyard....
But burial grounds are respected
And the soil dutifully
Returned to its original lay....
But here, a deathtrap....
The ground beaten and pounded....
Patches of garbage rots....
Dogs feast....
Where have we arrived?
Will it change?
Will we change?
Or has an inertia set in....
I think, somewhere along the way,
Many have lost their will....

*****

## ***The Beetle....***

I chanced upon this beetle,
It had turned upside down,
Frantically waving its little legs,
To stand up on his ground....

Toppled briefly on one side,
Then again, onto his shiny back....
The struggle seemed so endless,
But in his effort, there was no lack....

As slowly fades the glimmering light,
Exhausted, in need of a gentle breeze,
The beetle heaves to rouse once more,
With a kindly act in time of need....

A meagre pause just to breathe,
And the feat started again....
Then triumphed but ne'er gave up,
His labour was not in vain....

And so be it in one's time....
'Tis not the toil or strife,
But conviction....faith in yourself,
And belief in your life....

*****

## ***Existence.......***

I am an idea,
Or maybe a dream....
I am a thought,
Sometimes a prayer....
I am not yesterday, today
Or tomorrow....
I can be happiness
Or sorrow....
I am not master of my destiny,
Nor,
Of my fate....
I believe in goodness,
I am not hate....
I love to laugh
And cry....
I am daring, yet
Also shy....
I am not my fear,
I am the sound between a space,
I am the silence
In the core of every loud....
I cannot be everyone,
I am just one in a crowd....
I am the chances I take....
And the choices I make....
I am 'me' in many forms....
I am just a creation....
I came and shall be gone....
My identity cannot be defined....

I am an idea
Or maybe a dream....
I am a thought,
Sometimes a prayer....
I am and shall always be there....

*****

## ***The Old Banyan Tree.......***

Old as the soil first humoured my seed,
And the cascading downpour from the sky,
Nurtured by none other than the sun,
Unclad, a tiny sapling was I....

I do not remember, now old,
Older than all the tangled roots,
Ghosts resting on my laboured branch,
Serenaded by an owl's hoot....

The old banyan tree stood stoic,
Deep in the dirt of earth's bed,
Its roots hang like dreadlocks,
Encircled with holy threads....
Gnarled and knotted its aged trunk,
Storing secrets and many a tale,
From sunrise to sunset,
Every dawn and dusky pale....

The leaves flutter to die each year,
Only to be reborn once more,
There are no karmas in its memoirs,
Just the truth of time, gone by and yore....

Mellow in its sheltered shade,
Leaves upturned to kiss the sky,
Sometimes blue, then thundering black,
An ever protective eye....

I stood for a while and wondered,
As the sunlight rippled through,
Nests dappled on branches high,
While spring birds sang a few....

Entwined into a broken wall,
Creeping further to faded garden
Of no one's home....
Roots shall lurk into unknown ground,
Forever in a roam....

*****

## ***Dream With Me.......***

Come a while and dream with me....
On this tufted grass, as I lay,
A brightened sun finds its way,
'Neath the shade, as day takes flight,
Weaving stories that I keep,
Shhhhh.... do not tread them with your feet.

Wings I owned but they chose not to fly,
Oh, how I longed to reach that high,
Within a space where I did live,
I gave....had a lot more to give....
Not to myself but to those I had pledged,
And suddenly a lifetime had gone by,
My hidden wings forgot to fly....

Regrets, I have none,
For I have loved my best,
Perhaps tomorrow, while I rest,
I shall meander in a pause....in my time,
Come out from a hushed within to climb,
And learn to spread those veiled wings,
For then my hallowed song shall I sing....

Come a while and dream with me....
On this tufted grass, as I lay,
A brightened sun finds its way,
'Neath the shade, as day takes flight,
Weaving stories that I keep,
Shhhhh.... do not tread them with your feet.

*****

## *Faith....*

And Faith,
Was a name of this bonny child....
Be it the heat of May or rain of June,
She swirled and twirled to a lovely tune,
"Walk by my side or far away,
I shall hold your hand every day....
No stone shall shy my hope or trust,
Do not believe in me if you must,
But pray, do not run for a mere cover,
I shall defy all odds and win you over....
Remember my name is Faith...."

*****

## Let It Go……

Be kinder to yourself,
Leave what pains on the edges
And let it flow away,
Like water down a hill,
Let it go alone….

And you thought
You had lost yourself….
Nay….you shall heal….
The hue of today shall be
Another form of art tomorrow….
Let the silent chaos go,
Reach out….
But for your own hand….

Be kinder to yourself,
Leave what pains on the edges,
And let it flow away,
Like water down a hill,
Let it go alone….

*****

## ***Within Myself....***

I hear a murmur
Within myself....
Who else
But me....
Then why do l allow
Others to judge
What they cannot see....
So deep, deep inside of me....

Yet I get swayed
And appraise my worth,
Chain my thought....
For a while....
Dare to put myself on trial....
Who more foolish than I,
To let these interpretations
Not pass by....
The prison inside
Shall never free....
If I believe in
Orations of others speak....
It is then that I lose
Who I am,
For I live not my own....

Sitting inside, watching me,
Holding my spirit,
Someone spoke last night,
Whispered a tap....

Maybe the moonlight,
Sighing on my window pane,
Fluttering through a silent,
Shaking loose a flow of dreams,
Unlocking....
I felt a release....
It is then I remembered
What I had heard....
I saw myself in a clear....
Step aside....I am done,
I am not caged....
But liberated....I have won....

Within myself....
Who else
But me....

*****

## Global Warming......

And they slept in peace,
Those voices of the hills....
The calm of the sea,
Beloved brown of hearth,
And green of trees....
'Twas when the earth
Sang her tales....
Oh, perfect was the world,
It was a time when man bowed
In reverence.

Where is that sky, where is the blue?
The marauding haze has stolen its hue....
Thunder reigns the wrath of rain,
As lashes drown the soul in pain....
Silt chokes, 'tis a terror of change,
Be warned as seas rise again....

Kill those trees....hack them to death,
Burn the forest...the flower beds....
Gag their breath...scorch the years....
I am man....who you should fear....
I will build a life of ease,
I have only myself to please....

Alas, the beast did his best to roar,
Greed and lust, a want for more,

And earth became deathly silent....
Red waves lapped the sand....
Destroyed.....in agony, our motherland!!

But.....what about that child
Who is yet to come?
Who will stand by the unborn face to face?
Why are there skeletons in this race?
And tell the truth of your abuse,
Of corrupting shadows
And sobbing roots....

An infinity of a plastic dawn,
There will be an endless in the end,
A deafening echo,
Buried in a hope to mend....
And just before you fall asleep,
Dream of a sound that was once human
And believe, that this is no myth....
No dream....
A landscape of lethal screams....

*****

## ***Unsaid.....***

Voices that speak loud,
Sometimes, just inside the mind,
May feel the need to hide away,
Thoughts that are trying to find....
A way to come out and break free,
Because you really want everyone to hear,
Yet there is a part that's invisible,
Cloaked in fragments of unspoken fear.

These may be just tiny doubts to others,
But can turn into torments inside your head,
And reveals not in what you are saying....
But a lot of what is left unsaid.

I know many of us wear two faces,
One smiles and responds to all that is asked,
The other, eclipsed, trapped, not in view,
Is the face behind the mask.

* * * * *

## ***That Forgotten Family Home....***

Several years ago, the floods in Srinagar devastated my grandparents' home. Now, nobody resides there. Set against a background of a snow-covered landscape, it is prominent and poised in its historic dignity. 'They' were there until a while ago and then a sad perception of desolation framed the walls. The two dish antennas tell a tale, as do the broken window panes. The barren tree, in all its naked splendour (was it the walnut tree I remember so well?) stands as a permanent sentinel, as does the lone eagle perched atop it. Both majestic and proud against the winter white. There is a haunting quietness that speaks of a nobility lost within its sturdy, rustic bricks. This winter landscape is poignantly, almost eerily, divided by the wall behind the house.

Images of the past come to life, and I am reminded of searching through old items in the attic above the Villa, in the hopes of discovering some hidden treasure that may have been missed in the excitement of visiting my grandparents as a child. We are all emotionally connected to this proud house because of its rich history.

There is an ache in that house,
I can feel its pain,
Of those who have now gone,
Had once lain....
In all the splendour and glory,
That shone everywhere,
I search for it....
Through mangled wood,

But nothing there....
Drenched by the Jhelum,
Bruised by neglect,
Sorrowing in the loneliness
Desolate and bereft....
"You all stole my soul
And left me to die,
If my dirt walls could speak,
All would cry...."

Let it pass into hands,
That cares to revive....
It has a spirit, a will to survive....
There it still stands through
Many a strife....
Let it go....let it go,
Now this 'once a home',
Needs a new life......

There is an ache in that house,
I can feel its pain,
I can feel its pain....

*****

## *A Jasmine Garland and an October Song...*

Come, sit by me
While I bead the string....
The sun is out,
The clouds have taken flight,
"Don't go too early,"
I had told the rain,
"We need to hear the music
Of your story again...."
Leaves have cleansed
And among the bronzing fall,
There is a different aroma of dirt,
Little feet among the greenest grass,
Stay besides me, sweet morning earth....
And these are not beads....
But a sigh of jasmine buds,
They fell of this branch,
While an October breeze crooned,
And the blackbirds danced.

Come, sit by me
While I bead the string....
The sun is out,
The clouds have taken flight....

*****

## *Our Space......*

I have met many people
In this travel of my time....
Some were meant to be dear to me,
Some were not meant to be mine....
Yet paths crossed where
Our roads met,
A few came along....
Others went their way,
Those who were at a distance,
Were not there to stay.

At the end, nothing is ever wasted,
We have all moved at our own pace,
Grown through, in the unknown....
Rising, falling and rising again
In this....the freedom of our space....

*****

## ***A Wayward Stone.....***

I came upon a wayward stone....
It lay just there,
Lesser known
That my steps were not stumbling
But....
Maybe there was a reason
It came in my path,
I felt the pain of an aftermath,
As I tripped, yet picked myself up
From that fall....
Had I stalled?
For there, written on that stone,
Were words....
"You are not alone....
Your feet did err,
Each falter will make you wise,
I am placed there to make you fall,
Go down and then to rise...."

I once came upon a wayward stone....

*****

## ***Old Friendships.......***

Throw in a handful of vintage memories,
Treasures a little faded, a little worn,
A legacy of a familiar fragrance....
Even though threadbare or slightly torn....
A scoop of something old,
Something new....
Something bygone....
Something blue....

Perfect......
Is rarely full of charm,
Its allure does not captivate,
Fascination is in the flaws....
The beauty in a little blemish,
A small chip....a little blight,
Imperfection are those tiny cracks,
That lets in the light....

*****

## ***About That Bygone Home......***

I frequently pass this dilapidated old house. Its perimeter is touched by a main road. This outdated bungalow has always stood in this location, as far as I can recall. For the past twenty years, this is how I have observed it. On this continuously busy road, traffic moves back and forth, and everyone can't help but notice this disarray and ruin. Nobody even approaches it. I've never noticed a person near the abandoned, damaged building. Are there any stories? I have no idea because I have never asked. I'm sure the land and the plot's location are priceless, but no one is interested. The exterior, which is covered in overgrown grass and untamed weeds, has eroded the walls and is both an eerie, unsettling reminder of its past and a mysterious presence in the present. It now serves as a landmark. A sign indicating the path one is taking. I'm curious to know if anyone has had the nerve to enter. A few of these dilapidated homes, reminders of a bygone era, can be found scattered throughout the city. They are abandoned and lie undisturbed. Do ghosts and strange beliefs enshroud them? Superstitions prevent anyone from touching even a brick.

Walking past broken bricks
And distressed walls,
I look upon a bruised ruin
Where once lived, maybe,
Laughter, joy, and sorrow.
Curiously, I pause to decrypt
An old tale....maybe....

"Don't go in," a passerby warns....
His words a mere whisper
On a breath of wind,
It exhales,
Not so gently,
A gust blowing,
Slapping past an unhinged
Creaking shutter....

Uneasy is the light,
Filtering in through
Wounds in the stonework,
Pass the broken panes....
Was there a message in that window?
What lies behind?
Leftovers of forgotten memories?
Let it be unknown....
And the blanks remain unfilled....
Do we really need another story?

*****

## *We Are A Work in Progress....*

Are there perfect people?
Those little details
Put together,
Or picked apart....
Life rarely has perfection....
Look beyond that....
Those long conversations....
Full days and laughter that turn into dreams....

And the possibility that
Those dreams will come true....
There is a special kind of magic in
The strength within us....
For we are all a work in progress....
Life rarely has prefect people....
If the heart is willing....
Moments can be perfect....
Those dreams will come true....
For we are all a work in progress....

*****

## *Journey....*

Life's journey is never a straight line....
One day it's on top of the world....
The path is clear,
So we move forward....
Or....
It's the edge of a cliff....
A steep drop....
So we go around....get a little lost....
But whatever....whenever....
We arrive where we are meant to be....

*****

## Frangipani Rain.....Forgotten Graves

I came across an old graveyard one day, neglected, broken and overgrown with dried grass. I felt an emotion inside that I could not explain. I stood there and looked and felt an ache, for here lay people, souls, who laughed and lived and had been so dearly loved by those closest to them. It was sad to see them forgotten.

A quiet stroll through tree-shaded lanes,
The ground bedecked with fallen frangipanis,
Strewn in abundance....
Like pieces of the moon scattered on the grass....

Sharing the same earth,
A grave,
Much loved once,
Now in a solitary space,
Whispers its story of loneliness,
In silent conversations
With the surrounding trees,
They hear, branches bowing down....

This place may be forgotten,
Its bricks in crumble worn,
Dried flowers of decay, tossed in dirt,
Of petals strewn and torn,
But listen....
Lay an ear against the debris,
You will hear a comforting sigh,

Where the earth did breathe
And flowers lived,
And the sky had no broken cry....

As years passed with every sunset,
And winds blew away secrets
To a whispered place,
Timeless truth lay embraced in sleep,
Hidden, cloaked in this ghostly space.

Here, once a buried heartbeat lain,
In peace, between a quieter place,
A smell so soft....as centuries turn,
Warm memory of Frangipani rain....

*****

## *Two Figures....*

I came upon two figures,
One had a frown, the other a smile....
A darkened cape one did wear,
The other, colours, draped in style....

A roughened path ahead, it beckoned....
Both walked, but the gait was ne'er the same,
Tall and straight, one did walk,
The other head down, he blamed....

I can go no further....
The road ahead is rough,
The woods are dark, the stones they hurt,
The way is really tough....
There is a fog and there is no hope....
It's futile, I cannot see,
In anger, he tossed his darkened cape,
Turned back....
From there, he did flee.

Ahh.... said the other one....
It's dark but I see a light....
The stars fill the sky and the moon is full,
Will guide me through this night....
The fog will lift and I shall see,
To walk with the clearer way,
For I believe....I have hope

And I have trust....
Has seen me through till day.

For he knew, a power did dwell within him,
It would take life ahead....
Always move him onward,
And belief was a beacon....a strong thread.
Then faith did take over,
It walked in step by his side,
A torch through the darkest times,
Faith, forever dwells in 'I'....

*****

## *I Once Chanced Upon This Heritage of Old......*

Quiet tones, down an alley of
Forgotten stories....
Not told in words....
Cluttered, ageing
Gently fading....
Peeling walls of yore,
Speaking in a silent
Wistful tone,
Through mist filled mornings.

The crumbling walls and
Fragile bricks,
Painted....
Repainted in solitude of
Wistful poignancy....
A lost grace of bygone grandeur,
Isolated remembrance,
Forlorn....almost forgotten,
But alive to the soul
Of who once embraced
The art of elegance.

I am mesmerized by
This finesse of old....
Quiet tones, down an alley of
Forgotten stories....
Not told,
In words....

*****

## *Musty Noon....*

The unseasonal rain had just abated....
Languid lull of the fan
Gets me nodding....
And I hear a buzz....
'Tis the bumblebee,
Losing its way through my open window....
Were I to slumber...I think not!
For....unaware....
My lost companion may tangle its wings....
I still the blades and
Bear the heat as it finds its way out.

Did I save the creature from being hurt?
Maybe not....but....
To be trapped within walls
Of unwanted places....
I, too, may need a saviour
To set me free....
For it pains to have one's wings torn....
I want that we should be there for others....
For....
We are all creatures of the same world....
Big or small....
The need is to be there for each other....
This silence has taught me so....
Be it a bird nesting in my favourite porch light....
Let it be....
A spider's web between iron-grills....
Let it be....

A cocoon on a plant leaf....
Let it be....
This is home....
Wait a while....
If removed,
No place can be called a home....
No one should be lost.
So let's hold hands....
We are all creatures of the same world
Big or small....
The need is to be there for each other....
This silence has taught me so....

*****

## *The Tiny Gecko*

I see a gecko on the wall....
Meaning no harm....
Just taking refuge behind the curtain....
Others in the room shun its sight....
Kill it...get rid of it, I am told
I contemplate....
More frightened than the rest
The gecko goes still in fear....
There is a full moon outside,
The stars are shining bright,
And dogs bark....they are free....
A cloth in hand, I deftly catch it unaware,
How much of a monster can this tiny
Thing be....
Freeing it on the grass, I see a wild scamper....gone,
I think....
I do hope on a bad day
I, too, am saved and looked upon with the same kindness....
For the monsters live in our minds....

*****

## ***Streets of Calcutta....***

*(Photographs speak....)*
Clay idols line the streets
Of broken pace and toxic drains....
He crouches, oblivious to aching joints
And sore feet....
Mesmerized by his devotion
To paint 'Ma' before her immersion.

A lone trod of slow footsteps....
As the old man, pot-bellied, head down,
A piece of yellowed, cracked soap
Clasped in his palm,
It has to see him through a month....
And a roughened yard of cloth
Over his arm,
He heads to bathe himself
Before the trickle of water turns to a drip.

Then there are those
Of morning, gathering at a tea stall....
Watching with vacant eyes
All who pass by....
Bony arms, labouring to pull
A rickshaw down cobbled paths,
Pass graffiti adorned, paan stained wall,
Wondering whether his soiled cloth bag
Will jangle with coins....
Today, he needs rice to feed his family.
The day passes....

An old lady sits on a uneven ledge....
Plays with the broken strap
Of her well-worn chappal....
Sipping dregs
Of water from a discarded bottle....
She has a long way to walk....
A stray dog, her only audience....
Eyes her intently, hoping for a toss of feed.

The other side shows
An abandoned gaiety of street children,
Unaware of scraped knees and torn clothes,
Enthralled in imaginary games and
Whoops of joy....
Their innocence unaffected by
A fated grim present and future....
Milk cans clanging out of tune
Against the tyres metallic spokes,
He heads home to his shed of cows,
Meandering through this maze of cars
And a circus called traffic.

There by the footpath,
Juggling and mingling in a sea of humans,
Saffron, bedecked with ash,
Smeared on forehead....
Prayer beds rotating 'tween gnarled fingers....
Eyes in an intoxicated trance,
Faded blue turban wrapped around matted hair,
Religion, too, walks the street in a chant.

Bidi in hand....
A weather beaten face,
Aged well before his time,
Reclining by a broken brick wall,
A breather from the day's toil,
Just to scrape a living,
He has the strength to still smile,
With broken teeth and a wave
To odd passerby, who may have,
Along with him,
Struggled through the drudge and survived.

The noon turns into nigh,
Rinsed in the aftermath of a hazy glow,
Raindrops glisten, summer shower,
On red streaks of reflected lights....
Patterns on a tarred road leading home.

It says 'A day in the life on the streets of Calcutta'....
I but draw my inspiration
As I leaf avidly through pages
That brings alive my journey, as I
Live through the eyes of a photographer....

* * * * *

## *Trees.......*

They speak to the sky
Of secrets untold,
And guard the under
Of forgotten souls,
Each with a purpose,
The wise shall know,
The unsaid silent promise,
It whistles with the breeze....
I envy those who are free....
I behold the forest of trees.

*****

## *If It Were Not for Silence.....*

Quiet your mind
And within....
Only then shall you hear....

If it were not for silence,
No sound would be heard,
No words spoken would
Reach to touch your soul....
If it were not for silence
No bird song would
Make leaves dance,
Nor the cry of a broken heart echo....
If it were not for silence,
Sound would resound
Like tin pans on a wall....
Trapped, unable to find
A way out....
And oh, how would we know,
Between the sweet soothe
Of gentle vibrations
And tumult of jangle....

If it were not for silence,
Flutter of autumn leaves
Would be oh so quiet,
Rustle of cloth playing
Between feet
Would be a mere sight....
Patterning of rain on

Windows and roof,
Panting of breath
With hie of footsteps....
Crackle of wood fire
On a winter's night,
You would not hear....
Nor any whispers of sweet nothing
In your ear....
If it were not for silence....

*****

## ***Scars......***

We all wear scars....
Some are seen,
Some hidden away….
They all remind us of a journey.

Some shine from inside out....
They are scars we wear well
And are forever teaching us....
Leading us....
Let them shine....
Some bear a silent ache,
They echo as they heal....
Touching on twinge of hurt....
Maybe pain,
Protect them....
They are ghosts....
They helped us survive,
We learn from them....
We all wear scars....

*****

## *Sometimes......*

Sometimes....
The bridge is too high,
The water too deep,
And the land too far apart,
But you have the freedom to choose,
To turn around or take a try….
So....
Just talk to your whispering heart....
"Should I stay back and safe,
Where there are no twists,
Nor any difficult bends....
Or move ahead, rise and grow,
Take my chance to the very end."

*****

## Home......

While a vision of normalcy seeps in,
we realize,
that in this past one year
we have formed a deeper bond
with ourselves and our home,
and we understood
that 'home' is not just a place,
it is a feeling....
a creation....love....memories....
And under its roof
resides delicate sensitivity....
This awareness
will stay with us forever....

*****

## ***The Transgender....***

I was a mystery
To myself and a sin to others....
Was I a mere ghost,
Closed in a closet?
My mind screaming in a prayer,
To god to do right by me.

My identity, a question mark,
Sagging under the shame,
The burden of a caustic aftertaste
That lingers like a serrated saw in my mind,
Each time I come upon vicious encounters
Of a harsh description of normal.

I am not accepted....
Not as a person, with a heart as full as yours,
Not fitting into a body drawn by hands....
Pencil on paper....
Woman or man.
Born into a body I do not know,
My mouth is shut in front
Of those I yearn to love,
Do they really see me?
Or do I exist between cracks....
But I stay....
No one will truly know the price I pay.

*****

## ***Angels.......***

I sense a hand
On my back....
On my arm....
And a gentle stroke on my head.

I hear a voice,
Soft....
Silent....
A whisper that brushes my ear.

I see a vision inside
My heart....
My conscience....
It speaks softly to me.

We are angels....
We are guardians....
We are invisible....
But we are there....
Feel us....
Hear us....
See us....

We are here if you need us....
Always....
Reach out....

*****

## *I Feel........*

I feel sometimes
I'd like to get away
From myself....
From a mind that thinks,
A hundred thoughts
With every blink,
From a heart that feels,
Every pulse,
Every emotion,
Of someone else.

I have carried with passion
All that belonged elsewhere,
Given with devotion
My share,
My whole as a daughter,
As a wife,
A mother,
A grandmother,
As a friend.

I feel sometimes,
I'd like to get away
From myself....
Maybe just for a day,
So that I can play
A role so hidden away,

It's not lost....shall never be,
But carefully wrapped
As a gift to me.

I feel sometimes
I'd like to get away
From myself....

*****

## A New Year Resolution.....

Hey all....
Let us do all desired
And not wait....
Tomorrow may
Just be too late....
Mend bridges
Hug and spread a bit
Of cheer among all,
Pick up that phone
And call....

Hey all.....
Keep the mind free,
Forget old woes,
Write out all negativity
And throw....
So that we breathe easy,
Let us all take that chance
For....
My dear friends,
It's never too late to dance....

* * * * *

## *Finding a Poetry.......*

Umber, yonder the fallen leaves,
Burnished copper, gold,
Demure in forgotten vintage lustre,
Cracks in an old, tiled floor....
Fragments of old rustic bricks,
Walls weather beaten, time-worn, in fade,
Sprinkling gravely dust of onus,
Carrying a grievance in weight
Of all above it.

Parched, the soil of earthen clay,
And a tired face,
Pebbled riverbed running so dry,
Bent back of an age-old pace,
Vultures navigating a burdened sky,
A sky that holds the downwards,
Not to let go,
Forever carrying the falling,
Of a world rotating in slow....
I hear words, hear lyrics,
Everything speaks to me and you,
Poetry can spill from cracks
Of old walls too....

*****

## *We are All in it Together....*

In a quiet, unspoken way....
Aware of a feel,
Apart....yet together,
We all perceive,
That may not be felt,
But it is real,
Because there is that perception....
That's unsaid,
Yet a connection,
Keeping us all bonded,
In a quiet, unspoken way....

*****

## *It Has Nothing to do With Age.......*

When we all get a little weary
And our pace begins to slow,
Know that the silvery streaks of wisdom
Doesn't trouble us anymore.

That teasing, mischievous sparkle,
May not glint as it once shone,
Remember, we are all in it together
Yes....we are not alone.

Because when we hear that catchy number,
Our feet still gets a spring,
And a captivating sight,
Gives us a feel of zing.

We may turn a deaf ear,
And squinting doesn't mean we cannot see,
Rather, experience has taught us patience,
And cleverly, we let things be.

Ahhh... do not get judgmental,
We take a back seat by choice,
We are not taking over the youngsters space,
But there is still a 'boom' in our voice.

Though mellowed like the sunset,
Soft, with comforting glow,
But believe me....

The heart beats as a young one,
Though we may not show....

Nor are we going anywhere yet,
'Cause life has a lot to be lived,
So, we may be going, but not gone,
Oh, my dears....we still have a lot to give.

So let's sing a song of growing,
Add fun and laughter to this page,
We are moving along like everyone,
It has nothing to do with age!!

*****

## ***Soul Mates......***

She sat on a bench so wide,
With enough place to seat a stranger,
Who would sit and share a little time,
Not delve too deep into her mind,
Yet take away some sorrow,
Perhaps, return again tomorrow.

And sure enough, there walked a man,
Who hesitatingly sat on the edge,
With a cautious smile....
He took a while....
And offered his hand in greeting,
She smiled....but her eyes had a saddened look,
The silence that stayed was an open book,
And he understood her story.

She did not tell, but he knew,
Words are not always spoken,
What lies unsaid has a deeper feel,
Between souls that are awakened.

So....
He did not delve into her mind,
Yet, sat and shared a little time,
Eyes mirrored the inner self,

He offered neither solace nor help,
Just a vibe and fingertips touched,
Buried mute of a guarded hush,
He took away some sorrow,
To return again tomorrow....

*****

## ***Unburdened.....***

A babes hand comes empty,
Not a frown....brow devoid of clings,
As when we go....with just our souls,
Unfettered of everything.
So....
Live between every story,
Go places never been....
Add generous splash of magic,
Colour, what an eye has never seen.

Fly every gust of wind,
Sail on every ocean tide,
Shout to the world your excitement,
Dance with every ride....

Feel unburdened and unencumbered,
Just revel in the freedom of being alive,
For we own as little as a mere nothing,
As when we first arrived....

*****

## ***The Sacred Jungle Wild....***

Throaty roar that rasps the ear,
Through jungle wild
The trudge is deep....
A blood moon sways
To an uneasy breeze,
Silent, the earth exhales a wooing call,
Mysterious whispers of a night,
Barely visible to an eerie sight,
Of gleaming eyes peering
Between secrets of hidden,
Darkened foliage, not to be found,
Under, sometimes, silver beams,
Sometimes, a placidity of breathless sound.

I, in bewitched footsteps,
Soul slow, treading on undergrowth,
Of moss and muddy algae,
And hypnotized by the
Hunger of a mantis pray,
Unlocking neither secrets nor
An unknown code of jungle law,
My lips in quietude at all I saw.

*****

## ***Déjà Vu....***

I came upon this house of old,
It had a fragrance of wealth
But not of gold,
The richness in its aura
Told of birth and more,
Where souls had met
Long before....
The cobwebs spun like
Gilded silk,
And peeling walls
Spoke no ill,
Rather, they had a feel I had felt before,
A tenderness of comfort yore.

Yet, there was a Deja vu....
It tugged inside....
The aroma had an essence in hide....
Had I been here?

Who was I? Black or white?
Did my heart rest beneath this earth?
Can anyone tell by sifting dirt?
'Tis then I hear an anguished cry,
This hearth had an unknown sound,
Buried deep....way deep
Into the riddled ground,
What I had sensed was

An atonement of one
In a soulful wait,
For the dust of this earth
Does not discriminate.

*****

## ***She....***

She....
She is moonlight in all its gentle forms,
She....
Is the star that glows through your despair,
She....

Is the cloud that shades your mystics,
She....
Is the river that sensitively flows you to your destiny,
She....
Is the mountain that stands tall in shield,
She....
Is the chalice that collects your tears,
She....
Is the placebo for all your hurt,
She....
Is the sun for all your shadows,
She...

Is your strength,
She....
Moves like liquid fire....
Sensual....
But beware....do not kindle her ire,
She can burn....
She is grace....she is a warrior....
She brings into being a creation
Called life....
She....

* * * * *

## ***Belief.....***

A privileged man needs to see an image of God....bedeck him in finery,
And house him in a place of worship that is of comfort, before he has faith and belief.
Whereas a poor man sees the image of God even in a stone....
It may be under a tree, or by the side of a road, or his humble home....
It is his faith that makes him believe
God exists everywhere.
But....
All come to seek and ask....
The privileged ask not to lose all that they have....
The not so privileged ask for strength
To bear the losses.

* * * * *

## *Do Not Forget This Soldier........*

I dedicate this poem as a tribute.

A soldier has died many times and his passing is silent. Now, a tribute honouring his life must be heard by all! He does not care about the dread that hangs menacingly in the air while we fight our fears during this lockdown. His only protection is courage and love for his country.

Send me home wrapped in my tricolours,
By my coffin, they place a wreath,
But only my dearest near ones,
Shall truly cry at my feet.

Though others shall sing my praise
And lament that I have gone,
'Tis only the whispering wind,
Singing to me as I died alone.

Yet....
No thundering sounds awaken the skies,
No sea waves shall salute me home,
No band shall trumpet my bravery song,
When I died....I died alone.

Do not forget my bravery,
I ask for no applause,
But remember me as the one
Who silently embraced your life,
And died for a cause.

*****

## ***Pandemic of Fear......***

There once lived a monster....
It was fierce and controlled my mind,
But it was oh so invisible,
Impossible to find.

When least expected,
It would take over my head,
And I was told by an eerie voice,
It lived under my bed.
The night played with shadows,
On walls, sometimes my window panes,
Face under covers....one eye peeping out,
I thought I would go insane.

Anyway....
That was a childhood story,
Of niggling fears and bits of fright,
Of unknowns that stalked an innocent mind,
And manifested at night.

But now I am all grown up,
And have children of my own,
And do you know what....
That abominable monster
Does not leave me alone.

Popping up at all places,
Ambushing all sanity in my head,
It resides in every pitfall,

But has come out from under my bed.
Now I see it in different forms,
My imagination makes it appear,
Larger than life, hypnotic....
It resides in a word called 'fear'.

* * * * *

## ***Healed.....***

It will come
With a gentle stroke of a hand,
It will come
In the form of a prayer,
In acts of kindness
To all who have faith….

It will come to all
Who believe
It is there....
In the beauty of the stars,
The bird song, or in a beam of light,
It is there
In your soul....in the feel of life,
It is there
In your beauty
Within and out,
And you should behold
That to reach this light,
You have walked through darkness,
And as you walk this path,
Know that you have healed.

* * * * *

## *Hope*

Hope is a word,
A thought,
A faith,
A prayer....
Hope is an expectation,
A probability,
A suspense,
A dream....
Hope is contemplation,
A wish,
An appeal,
An ache,
A motivation....
Hope is a quiet, subtle light....
The glimmer is there,
An aura, a shaded radiance,
And it will shine through.

*****

## The Search.....

I searched everywhere,
During cold mornings in the crisp air,
Through fog that mists ghost like trees,
Trodden treasures of bronzing leaves,
Fragments of sunshine
Between breaking beams,
I searched for answers in my dreams.

Mountains high that I would climb,
To speak to the moon
And stars that shine,
In the precious dirt that savours again,
Each blade of grass, each drop of rain.

I searched in darkness
Where I could not see,
That the light I sought was within me.

*****

## ***Thoughts by the Roadside...***

I sit by the roadside,
On a wooden bench, barely wide,
Yet enough to take in
My myriad thoughts,
As I watch the little world around me
Go by....
I see a man walking at a slow pace,
His tread weary as he stills his gaze,
Eyes empty....
Oh, but they speak so much
That I can write his story....
He is so real in his sorrow.

Then....there on a browning patch
Of forgotten grass,
Under the canopy of a benevolent tree,
A girl wipes a wayward tear,
I inhale her tenderness....
How bravely beautiful is she,
To feel and explore so much,
And know of
How compelling is the sense of pain....
Its existence makes one realize
The reason for life....
And in her silence
She is so complete.

It is when I feel the loneliest,
That I am not alone,

I realize as I take in
And absorb all that I observe,
I am not weak,
After all we are but human,
Healing in our broken,
For I have compassion to feel,
The poignant and the beautiful,
And I too, am braver than I know.....

*****

## *Her Basket of Grace......*

Dew drenched morning
Of a clear blue sky,
She sits with a gentle smile on her face,
As the season mellows,
Among a wealth of colours,
Baskets of crimson, tangerine, yellows....

"Please take some and string them
To make a garland intertwined with white,
Place them on your pretty wrist,
Or laced through fragrantly oiled tresses,
Petals, sweet-smelling, delightfully light."

"Here....a circlet of orange
To adorn an idol's feet....
But do tread cautiously
On spreads of rajnigandha,
Strewed along cobbled streets.
I have yet to thread these blooms,
The day has just begun,
The parakeets fly with frolic,
And the koel has sung."

Spring celebrates the festive paves,
Caned baskets...jasmine and marigold, roses in red,
"My lady....you look forlorn....
Here, take a handful of joy and embed
It to cup your face and inhale

The aura of a perfumed vibe, that will envelope your very essence,
And imbibe the scent, that will make you smile yet again...."
As her day is done, and sunset kisses the horizon,
She gathers her wares,
A lifelong share
Of heartstrings, inside a woven basket on her hip....

Empty?
No, no, look again....
It has dreams, stories, wishes,
A little sadness, tragedy, hope,
Regrets and thankfulness,
Wrapped up in little packages of time....
Carried on a sauntering gait....
Each separated, yet together,
To become everything....

So....
When you see her selling love,
A sentiment, a homage, a verse, or a prayer....
Gather an armful of emotions
And lay them where
Her blessings reach....they are from her soul....
This lady....with her basket of grace.

*****

## ***Reflections.....***

Is my coat a little shabby?
And shoes a little worn?
Do my grey highlights need
A rinse of dark?
My hem a little torn?
Do those lines of joy
Laughter....tears
Bother me?
I think not....
They are my wealth....
A mild cough, sometimes a painful back,
A small price for my maturing health.

For in my lap lies a basket....
With flowers....some fresh,
Some slightly withered and old....
Yet their colours....powerful that
I see no flaw and
Fragrance intensely bold....
Each bloom, my child....my memories,
My relationships....my ups and downs....
Their petal soft....maybe a little fading,
Does erase away every frown....
I forget when the flowers were plucked,
And who laid them in my care,
I see not their blemish....
Some are drying here and there....
All I do is inhale a scent so inspiring,
Intense....alluring, negating the smallest sigh....

Removing every trace of trivia,
That may hurt the eye....
For there in that mirrored reflection
I see a smile for every pain....
The richness lies in not what may be lost....
But in the bounty of every gain.

*****

## ***Sunrise....***

Weightless in the morning sky,
All by itself....
Waiting to wake
And wash its soul with dew,
And colours break....
Falling through bit by bit,
Then alive....bigger than a dream,
And freedom....
So much with so little....
Where the earth meets the sky....

*****

## There....

There, among the crowd,
Is that figure that laughs the most,
Surrounded by a crowd of friends,
Plays a perfect host….
Yet alone in an isolated domain,
Withdrawn within empty walls,
Hiding aches they do not see,
No one sees the fall....

There....
Stands a fearless one,
Shielding all with utmost brave,
Being on the precipice,
Faultless in every save,
Yet alone on a solitary turf,
Fears rule every restless night,
Cowering even as a shadow falls,
Terror becomes a fight....

There.....
Stands generosity,
Handing alms to all in need,
A basket woven with many hues,
Small treats for those to feed....
Yet alone in a desolate corner,
With barely a morsel or cover to stay,
Asks for guidance away from greed,
Toil dominates the daily day....

Behind many a smile, there may be pain,
In acts of courage, hidden fright,
And a big heart may give to all,
Yet sleep hungry at night....

So life may not be your 'perfect'
And at times....
At times, envy may colour us green,
but not all 'perfect',
Either yours or mine, is as
Ideal as it seems....

*****

## *I Come Into This World Silently....*

I have come into this world....
I align with whatever
Life brings to me....
What stays away,
Is not meant to be,
And what is mine to be
Will find me....

I won't change,
I won't chase,
No matter how much I run,
I cannot catch
What is to be free....
I live with
Love, hate, anger, calm, joy and sadness...
Emotions of all kind....
I move with time....
I do not own it....
It owns me....

I come into this world silently....
And then
I go....

*****

## ***Make it Matter....***

Infinite is the world,
Yet our space is
A design....just in passing,
A creation....

This world
Is the lifetime given to us....
This world is
What we are
Connected to....
Attached to....
Relate to....
Emotionally....
Mentally....
Physically....in this span of our lifetime....

This world is
As far as
Our eyes can see....
Our hands can touch....
Our ears can hear....
This world is
What we
Taste....
Smell....
Sense....
Feel....
Imagine....
Identify.....in this span of our lifetime....

Our existence
Is just this space given to us....
We visualize it as very large,
We make it imposing,
And immense
In our expectation....
But....
The truth is....
Our frame is very small,
And we will realize that
When our time passes,
That our place is
Just the finite circle
Where we did belong,
But did not own....
This lifetime was given to us
In momentary....
Make it worthwhile....
Make it matter....

*****

## *The Soul Seeker....*

I delve into the unknown,
Timeless in its voyage,
There it goes....
Slowly in its flow
And is gone....
Waiting on wings to set you free,

So....
Seize the day, my friend,
Ask not too many a 'why',
For here and now....
What may seem far,
It's not so....
Just reach for the sky....
In all 'tomorrow' waits
The soul seeker,
Its clock keeps time....
Seize the day....each moment....
Carpe diem....Carpe diem....

*****

## *My Quiet Space....*

My quietness is my space,
And within that silent sound
I live in a lot of colour....
I lilt with a flow of words
And strokes of abundant hues....
My heart beats for the small things
That pass us by,
In the blink of an eye....

I watch, as each year
The munias build their nest
In a safe place,
Between my pots and plants,
And I can't
Stop marveling at their deftness,
In weaving a cocoon like home....
"Stay safe, little birds,
Yon crow is always on the prowl,
Watching, waiting on the branch
Of the Jack fruit tree....
Stay safe, little birds."

*****

## ***Sit By My Side....***

Come sit by my side,
Hold my hand for a while,
Let's look at the sunset
And just smile....
For a moment, let us forget the world around,
Close our ears and mind,
To a sadness of sorrowful sounds.

Come sit by my side,
Hold my hand for a while,
Let's look at the sunrise
And just smile....
Childhood friends and nonsensical joys,
Let us just talk of those happy plays....
Smell reminiscent aroma of bygone days,
You tell a joke and I will laugh along,
We will hum a one-time tune,
Sing old songs....

Come sit by my side,
Hold my hand for a while,
Let's look at the stars
And just smile....
I gather some lavender,
You sip your tea....
The world looks like a painting,
Breathe in the memories....

Come sit by my side,
Hold my hand for a while,
Let's look at the crescent moon
And just smile....
Let's never forget each other,
For we are different flowers,
Bound in a bouquet of connection,
Complementing every hour....
Every second....every minute,
That goes by....
Hold on to love of all little, big things,
Or gone....lest it should fly....

Come sit by my side,
Hold my hand for a while,
Let's dance in the pouring rain,
And just smile....

*****

## ***The Album....Passage of Time....***

Looking back over my shoulder,
I search in a crowd
For my bygone self,
I cannot find that familiar face,
The passage of time travelled is long,
Memories are like
Softly fading songs....
And distance between
Now and then, far....
Sometimes a quiet sigh
Softly slips by....
Moments....hues in sepia....
How time does fly,
Through that little window....
Trying to hold on....
Then,
Letting go....
You and me
And so many others....

*****

## ***Fearless....***

What would I do if I was never afraid….
Surf the breeze like an eagle in soar....
Colour my world like a garden in spring....
Walk the edge of a mountain high....
Drown all the ruckus with my sing....

What would I do if I was never afraid....
Walk at midnight in forest deep....
Cry like a baby for the world to hear....
Voyage the oceans, swim with the sharks….
And laugh….oh how I would laugh in the face of fear....

What would I do if I was never afraid....
Tell all the truths I need not hide....
Let all my wrinkles show....
Flaunt my greying hair to the hilt....
Let my aura glow....

If not afraid, then shall I be....
Walking with my head held high....
Get that tattoo....dam the world....
Boogie my way up to the sky....

* * * * *

## *The Light Within....*

Go slow through that doorway
Fire sweet....
Do not burn to singe,
But spread a warmth
That awakens the soul to find
All....
Even illusions....
Do not let them die....
Nothing can be more sad
Than the silent crackle of dying embers,
Spreading a numbing cold inside....

What does not touch the heart
Is still beautiful if you love it....
And restful be the light....
The breath of a prayer....
Of spirits that come out....
Go slow through that doorway,
Fire sweet....
Do not burn to singe,
But awaken the soul to find
All....

* * * * *

## ***Forgotten Lanes......***

A morning walk
While the rain takes a break....
I meander through an untried path....
Just for the pleasure of finding
A new experience of gazing
At unknown stories....

I view an uncared for
Staircase, now not used....
Leading to nowhere,
And footsteps going up or down,
Have been long silenced....
A stairway to heaven?
The damaged home has no roof....

As I stroll, I spy a window
Who is watching me?
No one but a ragged cloth
Hanging on a hinge....
Its message clear….
There will be no one looking out.

Sauntering through empty shelters,
Caged in by old monuments,
Living with uncomplaining people,
Small talk full of dreams
Of big places,
An odd hawker peddling wares,
Unaware of a portrait where this

Small world is more bare
Than a vision of nothingness....

Finding a way out, I head back home....
It starts to rain....
And I wonder about those
Houses with no roof....
Forgotten lanes....

Yet truth be told....
We live side by side....
Ignoring these faded scenarios,
Pretending they are mere
Works of fiction....
The real world is only
What we want to believe....
Then I think....
'Empty is not nothingness....It is a space with infinite possibilities....'

*****

## ***The Rose Seller.......***

Red ones....yellow and orange....
She sells roses by the road,
Through weaving traffic
And blaring horns,
Her life on hold,
Bargaining down to the last rupee,
But lays that bouquet in your lap,
Barely counting the coins....
There is pride in her bearing,
That she did not beg or steal,
So why would you deprive her
Of a meal,
Just for a few more coins....
She does not sell flowers
But her right to live....
So please,
Those who decorate their fancy vase,
Give....
For....her heart is richer than yours....

Hair pulled back,
Smile on her scrubbed face,
Clothes withered, worn,
Like the old woman by the wayside,
Maybe her mother....
Who knows....
She sells roses by the road.

*****

## *September Nights.....*

The glorious night when all shall sleep,
Through sounds, the darkness hidden keeps,
Hums and echoes, branches creak....
Under the weightless hoot of the barn owl.

While a silver moon waltzes with the sky,
Flirting, winking with the stars in passing by,
I hear a soft croak of the frog amid lotus leaves,
While autumn bronze, laying on the ground, takes a heave,
To the tap dancing clicking beetles.

Cicadas and their eternal song,
Carried by a gentle breeze far and long,
I draw my laced curtains and while I breathe,
Untarnished pure the jasmine....fragrance of a flawless white,
Whispers of 'Clair De Lune'
Serenades the night....

Ahhhh....the glorious night when all shall sleep,
Through sounds, the darkness hidden keeps,
Hums and echoes, branches creak....
Under the weightless hoot of the barn owl.

* * * * *

## *And Sing You Shall....*

Keep walking....
In mind and feet....
Don't stop at a hurdle,
Move on....
Put one step
In front of the other,
And even though you are unsure,
Your path will find a direction,
You will find your way,
New opportunities will come by....
You may go through some days
Without a song, without colour,
But don't close your eyes,
Don't stop your hum
As you walk,
You will find your own picture....
You will find your own song....
And sing you shall......

*****

## ***Son Et Lumiere.....***

The stillness reverberated
With the cries of a myna bird,
"There is something I have
Been meaning to tell you,"
As I reach for the sky,
I see a wounded city and
The rivers run dry,
But rain is here and
My world will look
Greener than ever....

Perched on the window sill
Of a once upon a home....
White-washed walls,
Mapped with mildew,
Illustrate the drenched
Hues of the monsoon....
Soaked with changing lights,
Fragments shifting
While absorbing colours
Of morning, noon and night....
A neon sign here,
And a bright street lamp there,
Throws mottled, ghostly shadows
Of moving silhouettes,
In a 'son et lumiere' show....

*****

## ***Throw Not the Old and Used....***

They fascinate me....
Objects with old souls....
They have not died...
The pieces lie in sleep....
The poetry gently leans
Between the layers of their stories,
Memories of unseen things....
Even in the broken....
Faded by the light,
Treasured by many eyes,
The spirit of those who loved
These textures, are still alive
Within them....whispering....
In the rough and the worn....
Maybe a little torn....
Listen....
You can 'hear' them with your hands,
You can 'feel' them with your sight,
They are talking....reaching out....

*****

## ***Phoebe.....***

12th April 2023

Sometimes an encounter or a story touches one in such a way that you immediately want to pen it down. There is nothing extraordinary, but there are exceptional circumstances one chances upon, and some make you realize the worth of many good and positive things.

We had just experienced a bout of unseasonal thundershowers. Leaves and blossoms were scattered all over the ground. Broken twigs and fallen flower pots had made a mess. Armed with a cutter, I started trimming and removing all the clutter and tangles. As I was about to go back home, down the stairs came a lovely golden-haired 'Indie' dog. Buoyantly trotting through the porch, she gave me a happy sniff, wagging her tail. It was then that I noticed her front left leg was missing. I looked at the happy soul. She had adapted to the situation well and had obviously bounced back spiritedly.

Just then, a lady walked down the stairs. I inquired if she was the owner. She was. Then she went on to explain how she had rescued Phoebe, who had been hit by a speeding car, badly injured and her front leg crushed. The limb had to be amputated. "It took a while to nurse her but she was remarkable. Her morale was not to be quelled and here she is a couple of years later, healthy and happy."

It was so heartwarming to hear this 'happy ending' story. This lady had a kind and compassionate heart. I told her so. Phoebe is an inspiration. Strength of mind, patience and faith are so important. This lovely dog had the will to fight it through because she had the hand of a dedicated and passionate person soothing her traumas. My day was made....

*****

## ***A Prayer for a New Day......***

As a new day dawns....
Let all voices pray
For those who have lost their way,
And all who look for hope,
Let there be another day.

As a new day dawns....
Let those who hurt,
Feel for others,
A moment of their pain,
So that they may never harm again,
Soothe all those angry brows,
With a rose in one hand,
And a balm in the other,
So that they may never smother
A thought, a voice, a life.

As a new day dawns....
Let the air be cleaner than ever,
And all waters be clear,
Let heavens not weep in deluge,
Oh....never....
Let the earth not rumble to destroy,
And mountains not spew in such heat,
Let no man lay his life down in defeat.

As a new day dawns....
Let all those who do not care, also see,
That they too will leave behind a legacy,

For all pass on and shall give a future to
Those who come from within,
All love....even that man who sins.

As a new day dawns....
Let all houses of prayer
Be as one,
And every hand that prays
Carry the faith
And a message of humanity,
Let the new day bring
Peace and love,
For all eternity,
As a new day dawns....

*****

## *The 'Year' is Leaving....*

The 'year' is leaving
In a slow.....
The last daylight is going,
Let it go....
Open the doors, windows
Goodwill and grief need
A way out and in,
Hand in hand,
Thus, it has forever been....
'Tis not I who can wish for one
And will the other away....
Time has served both,
They come to leave or stay....
So let all live such,
So as to celebrate another day.....

The 'year' is leaving
In a slow.....
The last daylight is going,
Let it go....

*****

## *First of January 2024*

A long meandering, intricate road,
And traverse maybe tough,
Do not get lost, my friend,
Through the rugged and the rough....

Find your way home,
A lantern hangs above the door,
Its light illumes... steady the golden flame,
Tread gently on the rustic floor....

Be it snow or summer heat,
Gentle rain or autumn sleep....
A waiting hand strikes the match,
To torch a glow and vigil keep....

To home and hearth of this land,
Should you return one day,
Darkness will never stall your steps,
Yon lamp, frosted with age,
Shall ever guide your way.

*****

www.ingramcontent.com/pod-product-compliance
Lightning Source LLC
LaVergne TN
LVHW041156150826
845673LV00001B/179

* 9 7 9 8 8 9 3 6 3 4 0 8 2 *